National 4 & 5

History

The Making of Modern Britain 1880–1951

Claire Wood

Series Editor: John A. Kerr

HODDER
GIBSON
AN HACHETTE UK COMPANY

The Publishers would like to thank the following for permission to reproduce copyright material:

Photo credits

p.1 © Bert Hardy/Picture Post/Getty Images; p.5 © Mary Evans/Peter Higginbotham Collection; p.6 © National Museum of Scotland; p.11 © Mary Evans / Peter Higginbotham Collection; p.13 © English Heritage/HIP/Topfoto; p.14 © Pictorial Press Ltd / Alamy Stock Photo; p.19 © National Museum of Scotland; p.20 © RDImages/Epics/Getty Images; p.21 Salvation Army Social Campaign propaganda poster, London, c.1910 (chromolitho), English School, (20th century) / Private Collection / Bridgeman Images; p.26 © Illustrated London News Ltd/Mary Evans; p.27 © The Art Archive / Alamy Stock Photo; p.33 Mary Evans Picture Library/Pump Park Photography; p.39 © Pictorial Press Ltd / Alamy Stock Photo; p.43 (top) © GL Archive / Alamy Stock Photo, (bottom) © Punch Limited; p.50 © Mary Evans Picture Library/HENRY GRANT; p.57 © Hulton Archive/ Getty Images; p.58 © Punch Limited; p.59 © Punch Limited; p.64 © Hulton Archive/Getty Images; p.65 Lloyd George is used as a punch bag by both mistress and her maid, united in opposition to his National Insurance Act, 1911 (litho), Partridge, Bernard (1861-1945) / Private Collection / Bridgeman Images; p.66 © Illustrated London News Ltd/Mary Evans; p.68 Wikipedia Commons (https://en.wikipedia.org/wiki/Wikipedia:Text_of_Creative_Commons_Attribution-ShareAlike_3.0_Unported_ License); p.69 (left) "Never mind Bill, we're insured!" (colour litho), English School, (20th century) / Private Collection / © Look and Learn / Elgar Collection / Bridgeman Images, (right) "I don't care how often I get hurt now, I am insured" (colour litho), English School, (20th century) / Private Collection / © Look and Learn / Elgar Collection / Bridgeman Images; p.75 © Punch Limited; p.86 © Topical Press Agency/Getty Images; p.87 © Keystone/Hulton Archive/Getty Images; p.91 (top) © IWM via Getty Images, (bottom) © National Museum of Scotland; p.93 (top) Planet News Archive/SSPL/Getty Images, (bottom) © David Low, Evening Standard, 11 September 1940 via British Cartoon Archive, University of Kent, www.cartoons.ac.uk; p.95 © Fox Photos/Hulton Archive/Getty Images; p.103 © Pictorial Press Ltd / Alamy Stock Photo; p.111 © Topical Press Agency/Getty Images; p.119 © David Low, Evening Standard, 9 December 1948 via British Cartoon Archive, University of Kent, www.cartoons.ac.uk; p.120 (left) © Hulton Archive/Getty Images, (right) © J. Wilds/Keystone/ Getty Images; p.127 © Monty Fresco / Stringer/Getty Images; p.129 © Hulton-Deutsch Collection/CORBIS; p.130 © Albert McCabe/Evening Standard/Getty Images; p.131 in public domain; p.132 © David Low, Evening Standard, 19 July 1943 via British Cartoon Archive, University of Kent, www.cartoons.ac.uk.

Every effort has been made to trace all copyright holders, but if any have been inadvertently overlooked the Publishers will be pleased to make the necessary arrangements at the first opportunity.

Although every effort has been made to ensure that website addresses are correct at time of going to press, Hodder Gibson cannot be held responsible for the content of any website mentioned in this book. It is sometimes possible to find a relocated web page by typing in the address of the home page for a website in the URL window of your browser.

Hachette UK's policy is to use papers that are natural, renewable and recyclable products and made from wood grown in sustainable forests. The logging and manufacturing processes are expected to conform to the environmental regulations of the country of origin.

Orders: please contact Bookpoint Ltd, 130 Park Drive, Abingdon, Oxon OX14 4SE. Telephone: (44) 01235 827720. Fax: (44) 01235 400454. Lines are open 9.00–5.00, Monday to Saturday, with a 24-hour message answering service. Visit our website at www.hoddereducation.co.uk. Hodder Gibson can be contacted direct on: Tel: 0141 848 1609; Fax: 0141 889 6315; email: hoddergibson@hodder.co.uk

© Claire Wood 2016

First published in 2016 by
Hodder Gibson, an imprint of Hodder Education,
An Hachette UK Company
2a Christie Street
Paisley PA1 1NB

Impression number	5	4	3	2	1	
Year	2020	2019	2018	2017	2016	

Cover photo © Kurt Hutton/Picture Post/Getty Images
Illustrations by Integra Software Services Pvt. Ltd., Pondicherry, India
Typeset in 10/11pt Folio Light by Integra Software Services Pvt. Ltd., Pondicherry, India
Printed in Slovenia

A catalogue record for this title is available from the British Library

ISBN: 978 1 4718 5252 7

Contents

Preface   iv

The Assignment: what you need to know   v

1   Introduction   1

2   What was Britain like by 1900?   4

3   Why was there a problem with poverty by 1905?   10

4   What were the attitudes towards poverty before 1906?   17

5   Why did the surveys of Booth and Rowntree cause changes in attitudes to poverty?   25

6   Why did concerns about the Empire cause changes in attitudes to poverty?   32

7   Why did political changes help cause the Liberal reforms?   38

8   How successful were the Liberal reforms at helping children?   48

9   How successful were the Liberal reforms at helping the elderly?   55

10   How successful were the Liberal reforms at helping the sick and the unemployed?   62

11   What opposition did the Liberals face in carrying out their reforms?   73

12   To what extent did the Liberal reforms solve the problem of poverty?   78

13   What happened to welfare reform between 1914 and 1939?   85

14   What was the impact of the Second World War on welfare reform?   90

15   What was the importance of the Beveridge Report?   101

16   How successful were the Labour reforms at solving the problems of 'Want' and 'Idleness'?   108

17   How far did the Labour welfare reforms solve the problem of 'Disease'?   117

18   How successful were the Labour reforms at solving the problems of 'Squalor' and 'Ignorance'?   126

19   How successful were the Labour reforms?   137

Glossary   144

Index   147

Preface

This is one of a series of seven titles for the National 4 & 5 History courses to be assessed from 2014 onwards. Students should study three main units in National 4 & 5 History, with a very wide selection of topics to choose from (five in the first two, ten in the third). This series covers at least two topics from each unit.

The seven titles in the series are:

▶ National 4 & 5 History: Migration and Empire 1830–1939
▶ National 4 & 5 History: The Era of the Great War 1910–28
▶ National 4 & 5 History: The Atlantic Slave Trade 1770–1807
▶ National 4 & 5 History: Changing Britain 1760–1900
▶ National 4 & 5 History: Hitler and Nazi Germany 1919–39
▶ National 4 & 5 History: Free at Last? Civil Rights in the USA 1918–68
▶ National 4 & 5 History: The Making of Modern Britain 1880–1951

Each book contains comprehensive coverage of the four areas of mandatory content for National 5 as well as guidance and practice on assignment writing and assessment procedures.

The Assignment: what you need to know

National 5

What is the Assignment for National 5?

The Assignment is an essay written under exam conditions and then sent to the SQA to be marked. It counts for 20 marks out of a total of 80, so doing well in the Assignment can provide you with a very useful launchpad for overall success in the National 5 exam.

What can I write about?

You can write about a question linked to this book or something from another section in the course. In fact, you can write about any historical topic you want. You can even do your Assignment on local history.

What should I write about?

If you decide to do an Assignment based on the content of this book, here are some *good* possible questions:

✔ How significant was the problem of poverty before 1905?
✔ How important was the attitude of self-help before 1905?
✔ How far can it be argued that the surveys of Booth and Rowntree caused the Liberal welfare reforms?
✔ To what extent did concerns about the Empire cause the Liberal reforms?
✔ How far can it be argued that the Liberal welfare reforms were successful at helping children?
✔ To what extent did the Liberal reforms, 1906–11, solve the problem of poverty?
✔ How significant was the Beveridge Report, 1942?
✔ To what extent did the Labour welfare reforms, 1945–51, meet the needs of the British people?

What follows are *bad* titles for an Assignment:

✘ The problem of poverty before 1905
✘ Self-help before 1905
✘ Causes of the Liberal welfare reforms
✘ The Liberal reforms, 1906–11
✘ The Beveridge Report, 1942
✘ The Labour welfare reforms, 1945–51

These are just headings. You must have a question so that you can answer it. The bad choices would just result in telling a story.

Be safe! There are no prizes for giving yourself a difficult question that you have made up yourself. Choose something from the history you have already been studying. Avoid doing something risky – you only get one chance at this Assignment.

How long should my Assignment be?

Your Assignment has no set length – it is what you can write in 1 hour. Most essays are about four or five pages long.

What skills must I show I am using to get a good mark?

- You must choose a question to write about. That means your title should end with a question mark. Don't just write a heading down because you will just start writing a story or a project. Your teacher is allowed to give you a little help to make your choice.
- Collect relevant evidence from *at least* two sources of information. For example, these could be two books or one book plus an interview.
- Organise and use your information to help answer your question.
- Use your own knowledge and understanding to answer the question that you have chosen.
- Include *at least* two different points of view about your question in your answer.
- Write a conclusion that sums up your information and ends by answering the question you started with.

Remember that you also have a Resource Sheet to help you

On your Resource Sheet you will write out the sources that you will refer to in your essay. This will show the marker that you have researched, selected and organised your information.

Your Resource Sheet will be sent to the SQA with your finished essay. You will not be given a mark for your completed Resource Sheet but markers will use it to see that you have done the necessary research and have found appropriate sources to use in your Assignment. There is no time limit for completing your Resource Sheet and there is a 200 word limit, however your Resource Sheet must be written on one side of A4 paper. The Resource Sheet is *yours*. You can change it, colour it or print it out. You can write it anywhere, anytime before you write your Assignment under exam conditions.

National 4

The Assignment lets you show off your skills as you research a historical issue. You have a lot of choice in what you can find out about and you can also choose to present your findings in different ways. That means you don't have to write an essay to display your skills, knowledge and understanding.

To be successful in National 4 you have to show you can research and use information by doing the following things:

- Choosing an appropriate historical theme or event for study. Your teacher can help you choose.
- Collecting relevant evidence from *at least* two sources of information.
- Organising and using the information that you have collected to help you write about the subject you have chosen.
- Describing what your chosen subject is about.
- Explaining why your chosen subject happened (its cause) or explaining what happened next because of your chosen subject (its effects).

As you work through this book you will make mobiles, give presentations, and create posters and artwork. All these things could be part of your National 4 Assignment. You then have to present your findings.

Don't worry – if you get stuck your teacher is allowed to give you help and advice at *any* stage as you do your Assignment.

Do I have to write a long essay?

No, you don't. You can choose how you present your Assignment. You could do a talk and then be asked some questions about your subject by your teacher. You could do a PowerPoint presentation or keep a learning log or design a poster or some other way to display your work. You could even write an essay if you wanted to!

What kind of title should I choose?

The best advice is to choose a topic or event you are interested in. With advice from your teacher, you should make this into a question about the causes *or* impact of the historical topic. Here are question stems you could use:

▶ 'Why did …?'
▶ 'What was the impact of …?'
▶ 'What were the causes …?'

For example: 'What was the impact of the Liberal reforms on poor people?'

What information should I use?

You need to collect information from *at least* two sources of information. These sources can be primary or secondary.

Your information can come from written, visual or spoken sources. Useful information can usually be easily found in:

▶ textbooks
▶ websites
▶ television programmes
▶ local libraries and museums.

Keep a record of your progress in a log book or your work folder. Your teacher will help you with this.

How do I put my assignment together?

Once you've done your research, you need to make sure that you put your findings together in a way that will make sense to someone reading it. You have to give a certain amount of information and show your historical skills. Here is a suggested template to help you:

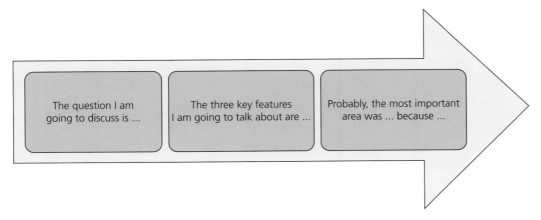

The question I am going to discuss is …

The three key features I am going to talk about are …

Probably, the most important area was … because …

Introduction (optional)

For example, if your question was: 'What was the impact of the Liberal reforms on poor people?' you could say:

My question is 'What was the impact of the Liberal reforms on poor people?' The three impacts I am going to talk about are the reforms for children, the old and the sick. Probably the most important impact was on children because the Liberals passed a lot of reforms for them.

Main part (necessary)

Discuss each of your three key features, using this template:

Key Feature 1 (Cause/Impact)	• Point of information to describe the cause or impact. • Point of information to describe the cause or impact. • Link back to question.
Key Feature 2 (Cause/Impact)	• Point of information to describe the cause or impact. • Point of information to describe the cause or impact. • Link back to question.
Key Feature 3 (Cause/Impact)	• Point of information to describe the cause or impact. • Point of information to describe the cause or impact. • Link back to question.

Conclusion (optional)

Overall, the most important cause/impact was …

This key cause/impact was important because … (give at least one reason)

How will I be assessed?

There are six skills you have to show in your assignment. These are:

◗ choosing an event or theme to research
◗ collecting relevant evidence
◗ organising the information to explore your chosen event or theme
◗ describing and explaining key features of your chosen event or theme
◗ describing the causes **or** impact of your historical event or theme
◗ presenting your findings on your chosen historical event or theme.

Remember, you don't have to do a long essay, even if you choose to write your assignment. You can also do a talk, PowerPoint or present an information poster. Your teacher will help you choose the best format for you. Good luck!

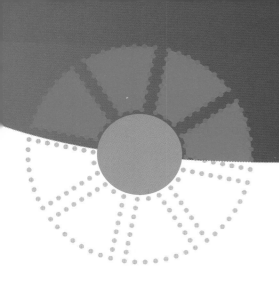

Chapter 1 Introduction

What is this course about?

SOURCE 1.1

Look at the picture.
1. How can you tell this child is poor?
2. Why do you think this child might be poor?
3. 'Think, pair, share': What help should be given to this child?

A child plays in an alley in the Gorbals, Glasgow, circa 1948

Today we take it for granted that social services will help us if we have unexpected problems or an illness. We would react in shock and disgust if social workers failed to protect the most vulnerable in our society. It is not only in times of crisis that we expect help from the government. We get help at all stages in our lives:

▶ Most of us are born in a hospital provided by the government and pay nothing for the treatment of mother and baby.
▶ Most of us go to schools provided by the government and pay nothing for the education provided.

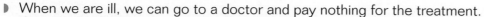

- When we are ill, we can go to a doctor and pay nothing for the treatment.
- If we lose our job, we can get help to find another job and financial support from the government while unemployed.
- When we are too old to work, we get a pension every week from the government to help us in our old age.

However, at the end of the nineteenth century people thought differently. They thought that if you were poor, it was your own fault, and it was up to you to look after yourself and your family. There was almost no help from the government or local authorities. There was no feeling of collective responsibility. This was the idea that everyone in a country should in some way help to support those people who had fallen on hard times.

Poverty means a person is unable to afford the basic needs of life. These 'needs' could include food, housing, heating and clothing. People who don't have these things are described as living below 'the poverty line'. However, whether someone is classed as poor can vary depending on the time being studied and the country being looked at. What it meant to be poor changed greatly in Britain between 1880 and 1951.

This course is about how and why attitudes to poverty changed. Then we will look at what governments did to help people in need. In particular, we will focus on the work of the Liberal Government, between 1906 and 1914 and the Labour Government between 1945 and 1951.

In this book you will read a lot about the Welfare State. It means that the **state** (otherwise called the government) looks after the **welfare** (or the health and wellbeing) of the people living in the country.

By 1951, most of the social services that we now call the 'welfare state' had been set up. The effect of the welfare reforms of the Liberal and the Labour Governments went way beyond just giving people money to get them out of poverty. The reforms created a mindset in which people increasingly came to expect governments to step in and sort out problems in all areas of people's lives, not just their physical needs. In doing so, the welfare reforms were vitally important in creating modern Britain.

What will this book help me to do?

This book will help you to be successful in your National 4 and 5 History course. It contains everything you need to know about the unit called 'The Making of Modern Britain, 1880–1951'.

This book provides advice and examples to help you answer questions to meet N4 and N5 unit assessment. There are a variety of approaches to N4 and N5 unit assessment in this book, based on source evidence in the chapter and questions at the end of the chapter. There are also practice questions for the National 5 exam.

Finally, this book will provide guidance to help you work on the Added Value Assignment tasks.

Introduction to tasks

This book aims to support you in preparing learners for unit assessment and course assessment. It offers flexible approaches based on meeting learners' needs.

How does this book help me with Unit assessment?

Unit assessment

All unit assessment tasks should be carried out under the supervision and control of assessors. The aim of unit assessment is to gather evidence of a learner's skills at each level. Therefore, learners can have access to their materials and notes during unit assessment. The time taken to complete the unit assessment should be negotiated with learners, based on their needs. This book offers several approaches to unit assessment:

Portfolio approach

These are tasks embedded within chapters. The tasks are day-to-day activities that would be completed as part of normal class work. Each task is aligned with one or more assessment standard. Learners can choose to do either N4 or N5 tasks.

Throughout the book, more than one opportunity will be given to learners to provide evidence that they meet the assessment standard. This approach often helps support positive achievement for learners working towards N5 or learners who find it difficult to access larger scale written assessments. Evidence from learners can be provided in oral, visual or written format.

You could also adapt the Learning Activities at the end of each chapter for the Portfolio approach to unit assessment.

When using this approach, assessors should take care to collect evidence of learners meeting unit assessment standards as they are met. For example, digital photographs can be taken of evidence from a workbook or work file. This information should be stored securely in line with local ICT policies.

Further advice and exemplars on how to use this approach can be gained from N4 and N5 Unit Assessment Support Pack 3 from the SQA Secure Area. Your SQA Co-ordinator will be able to provide you with materials from this part of the SQA website.

Unit-by-Unit approach

These are the tasks at the end of chapters for N4 learners. Normally, assessors would use these assessment tasks after learning and teaching. N5 tasks can be adapted from course assessment tasks. Further advice and exemplars on how to do this can be gained from Unit Assessment Support Pack 1 (UASP 1): N5 British from the SQA Secure Area. Your SQA Co-ordinator will be able to provide you with materials from this part of the SQA website.

Combined approach

Evidence from the British unit assessment tasks can be used to meet the assessment standards from Outcome 1 for the Scottish, and European & World contexts. Combined unit assessment tasks can be a useful way to reduce assessment for learners.

Further advice and exemplars on how to use this approach can be gained from N4 and N5 Unit Assessment Support Pack 2 from the SQA Secure Area. Your SQA Co-ordinator will be able to provide you with materials from this part of the SQA website.

How does this book help me with course assessment?

Tasks and advice have been provided at the end of every chapter to help learners prepare for the N5 exam.

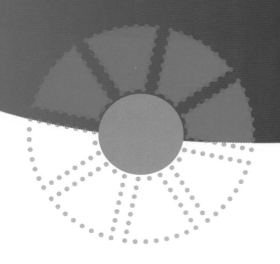

Chapter 2 What was Britain like by 1900?

What is this chapter about?

This chapter is about what Britain was like at the end of the nineteenth century. You will find out about the positive and negative impact of industrialisation on Britain.

By the end of this chapter you should be able to:

▶ Explain why Britain was a rich and powerful country.
▶ Describe how Britain was ruled.
▶ Explain why people in Britain were worried about the economy and poverty.

Why was Britain so rich and powerful?

SOURCE 2.1

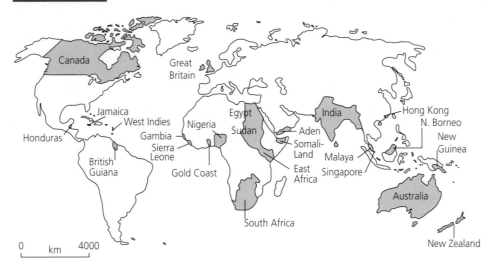

The British Empire at the end of the nineteenth century

Britain had control of a large empire, with land all across the globe. A powerful navy controlled the seas across which British ships traded. The navy ensured that no other country was able to seriously challenge Britain's power.

Another reason that Britain was so wealthy and powerful was because she had been the first country to industrialise. This meant that a wide variety of products and goods were now made in factories in Britain and were much cheaper to buy. An example of an industry that industrialised is textiles. Historians call the change in how things were made 'The Industrial Revolution'.

The Industrial Revolution brought wealth and importance to Britain. Some people became extremely wealthy. There was a growing middle class of merchants, bankers, ironmasters and factory bosses, but most of the population were still working class. Within this group there were large differences. Skilled workers such as engineers and craftsmen lived well, but unskilled labourers did not. Most workers were very poor and lived in poor housing. This was because wages were low and the industrial towns were crowded with all the people that had moved there looking for jobs.

SOURCE 2.2

This photo shows the poor housing that many people lived in. Overcrowding was common and housing conditions caused diseases to spread easily.

Activity 1

Look at Source 2.2. Describe two ways in which housing in Glasgow was poor at the end of the nineteenth century. (N4 British AS 2.1)

SOURCE 2.3

Compare the housing in Sources 2.2 and 2.3. You should find at least two differences.

'The Lee' Edinburgh, circa 1900

How was Britain ruled?

Britain was a **constitutional monarchy**, which meant the head of state was the Queen or King. However, monarchs did not have real power. This power resided with the two Houses of Parliament; the House of Commons and the House of Lords. British politics was dominated by the Conservative and Liberal parties during the nineteenth century. This changed as more men were given the vote in General Elections. The Labour Representation Committee (the Labour Party from 1906) emerged in 1900, as a result of more working men being given the vote. By 1900 two out of three men had the vote.

> **GLOSSARY**
>
> **Constitutional monarchy** a country that is ruled by a king or queen, but run by an elected government

What was the role of government?

Unlike today the government had a very small role in everyday life. It concerned itself mostly with defence and foreign policy. By 1900, the social problems resulting from industrialisation had forced the government to have limited involvement in the lives of ordinary Britons:

- Some health and safety control of the workplace.
- Setting of minimum standards of public health.
- Provision of limited education through local **parish** boards.
- Limited help for the poor in society classed as 'deserving' of being helped.

> **GLOSSARY**
>
> **Parish** an area of Britain based around the local church

Why was Britain worried about the economy?

Britons were very proud of being the leading world power for much of the nineteenth century. However, towards the end of the nineteenth century, Britain faced economic problems.

There were times when unemployment increased due to a decrease in trade. An important economic depression happened in the 1870s and 1880s due to increased competition from the United States of America and Germany. These countries industrialised later than Britain, but took advantage of the fact that they had up-to-date technology and vast natural resources. Britain was doing well, however, her competitors were growing faster.

By the 1890s, Britain had not managed to keep up with technological developments and new industries like the production of chemicals. This threat to her economic power worried people at the time. They wondered what had caused it and what could be done to make sure that Britain remained powerful. The diagram in Source 2.4 shows Britain's relative decline.

SOURCE 2.4

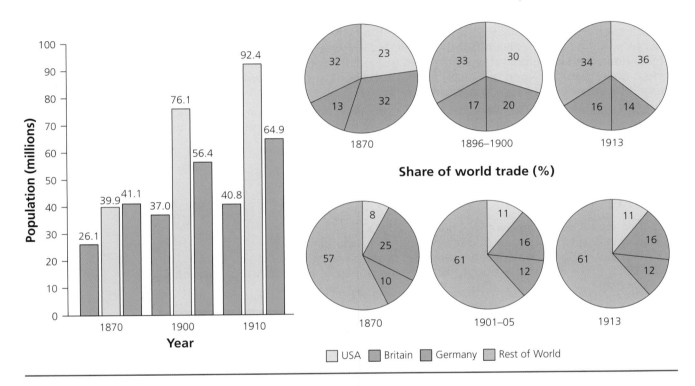

Activity 2

Look at Source 2.4. Describe at least three ways (or two explained points) in which Britain declined as a world power by 1913. (N5 British AS 2.1)

Why was Britain worried about poverty?

By 1900 a number of books had been published that described in great detail how the poor lived. These books were widely read by educated Britons. What they read horrified them. People wondered about how much poverty existed in Britain and what this meant for the country. There was speculation that poverty was a reason why Britain was falling behind her industrial rivals. Some began to think about what the government should do about poverty. In 1883, Rev. Andrew Mearns published a book called *The Bitter Cry of Outcast London*. Below he describes the dreadful poverty that led to appalling living conditions.

SOURCE 2.5

*Every room in these rotten and **reeking** tenements houses a family, often two. In one cellar a **sanitary inspector** finds a father, mother, three children, and four pigs! In another room a man was found ill with smallpox, his wife just recovering from her eighth birth and the children running about half naked and covered with dirt: seven people living in one underground kitchen and a little dead child lying in the same room. Elsewhere is a poor widow, her three children, and a child who has been dead thirteen days.*

> **GLOSSARY**
>
> **Reeking** stinking
>
> **Sanitary inspector** someone employed by the local council to inspect health and housing

Rev. Andrew Mearns, The Bitter Cry of Outcast London *(1883)*

Writers such as William Booth, the founder of the Salvation Army, had also begun to write about poverty. William Booth's book, *In Darkest England and the Way Out* (1890) described living conditions unknown to wealthy people. Britain was the richest country in the world but many people lived in dirty, overcrowded housing, begged for money and lived dreadful lives.

Although educated Britons were interested in poverty, most were unaware of how much poverty existed in their country. In fact, they had some strange ideas as to what caused poverty and what help the state should provide.

Chapter summary

- Britain was a rich and powerful country by 1900.
- This was due to its Empire and the Industrial Revolution.
- Within Britain there was great wealth and great poverty.
- By 1900 there was worry about the declining power of Britain and the increase in poverty.

Activity 3

Mind mapping

Put the heading: 'What problems did Britain face by 1900?' in your workbook or work file. Create a mind map of the main problems using the headings: 'Industrialisation', 'Economy' and 'Poverty'.

Question practice

NATIONAL 4

Source A is about the poverty of the Scottish working classes:

SOURCE A

Scottish houses were small with poor levels of lighting and sanitation. This was due to low wages and the fact that many Scots had jobs in industries like building where there wasn't work to be had all year round. This meant Scots could not afford better housing.

1 **Explain the reasons many Scots lived in poverty.** (N4 British 1.1; British/ Scottish AS 2.2)

Success criteria

You should briefly explain at least two reasons why Scots were poor.

NATIONAL 5

Explain why people were worried about the economy and poverty in Britain. (5 marks)

This is an 'explain' question. This means you must give five reasons why something did or did not happen. It is not enough to just write down facts no matter how correct they are. You must link each fact back to the question, explaining how that fact did or did not allow something to happen. For this question, this means that you need to explain why the economy and poverty worried people.

To get you started on your answer, here are some hints:

▶ Explain why economic depression worried people in Britain.
▶ Explain why increasing foreign competition worried people in Britain.
▶ Explain why Britain's failure to keep up with new technology worried people in Britain.
▶ Explain why Britain's population numbers worried people in Britain.
▶ Explain why Britain's share of world trade worried people in Britain.
▶ Explain why the rise in poverty worried people in Britain.

Success criteria

▶ Include five factual pieces of information on why people in Britain were worried.
OR
▶ Include at least three developed pieces of information on why people in Britain were worried.
▶ Give accurate and detailed pieces of information that are properly explained.

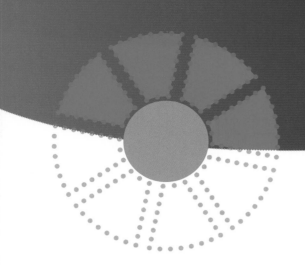

Chapter 3 Why was there a problem with poverty by 1905?

What is this chapter about?

By 1905, the problem of poverty had grown so much that some help had to be given. However, the help given was not the same across the country. Also, it was not successful at dealing with the problem. This chapter will look at the Poor Law system designed to tackle poverty.

By the end of this chapter you should be able to:

▸ Describe the Poor Law system in England/Wales and Scotland.
▸ Explain why the government used the Poor Law system.
▸ Explain why the Poor Law was hated.
▸ Explain why the Poor Law was not successful.

What was the Poor Law in England/ Wales and Scotland?

The system of help provided for the poor was based on the 1834 Poor Law Amendment Act in England and Wales, and the 1845 Poor Law Amendment Act in Scotland. The Poor Law operated a mixture of **indoor** and **outdoor relief**.

> ### GLOSSARY
>
> **Outdoor relief** help given to the poor in their own homes
>
> **Indoor relief** help given to the poor in a workhouse or poorhouse

SOURCE 3.1

- Parishes grouped into 'Unions' with a central *workhouse*
- Those in need of help had to prove they were poor. If they could prove they were poor they were allowed into the workhouse.
- Inside the workhouse, conditions were made so bad that they were worse than any conditions found in a poor person's own living place. This was called 'less eligibility'.
- The inmates were given jobs that were boring and repetitive.
- No help for the able-bodied poor was to be made available outside the workhouse. The able-bodied were expected to find work and look after themselves.

- Poorhouses were built and local Boards were elected to run them.
- The unemployed able-bodied poor had no right to help.
- Only the disabled, widows and deserted wives with children, orphans under 12 (girls) or 14 (boys), the old and sick could get help from the poorhouse.
- Poorhouses were not as harsh as the workhouse in England/Wales. For example, inmates were not forced to work.

Activity 1

Look at the Poor Law map of Britain (Source 3.1). Describe how the Poor Law worked in Scotland. You should make at least two relevant factual points or a single point which is explained more fully. (N4 British 1.2/2.2)

OR

Look at the Poor Law map of Britain (Source 3.1). Explain why people in poverty would not have liked the workhouse system in England and Wales. You should give at least three points or two points that are developed. (N5 British 2.1/2.2)

SOURCE 3.2

View of Lews Combination Poorhouse in Stornoway, Isle of Lewis. Built in 1894–96, it could house 66 inmates.

1 Why do you think someone living in poverty would not have wanted to live in a poorhouse?
2 Did this system deal successfully with poverty?

The short answer to question 2 is 'no'. The Poor Law had been designed to deal with poverty in the countryside. But by 1905, Britain was an industrial country with most people living in towns. The Poor Law could not hope to deal with the unemployment created when factories went out of business or there was a downturn in industry. The system simply could not cope with the scale of poverty in Britain.

The workhouse system was hated by the poor. Going into a workhouse was a humiliating experience. Workhouses were like prisons to many people. There was fierce opposition to workhouses in Wales and the North of England in particular.

What were conditions like in the workhouse?

Sometimes conditions inside the workhouses were exaggerated, but:

- The work provided for the inmates of the workhouse was boring and very repetitive.
- Families were separated in the workhouse. Children, adult males and females could not live together within the workhouse walls.
- The food did not vary and was based on cheap products. Meat was only given twice a week. The diet was often not enough. For example, in 1845 at a workhouse in Andover, starving **paupers** were discovered eating the marrow from the animal bones that had been supplied to the workhouse for crushing.
- Discipline within the workhouse was strict.

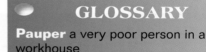

GLOSSARY

Pauper a very poor person in a workhouse

Charles Chaplin remembered going to the workhouse as a boy. He was born in 1889 in Lambeth, an area of London, and later he became a world-famous silent movie star.

SOURCE 3.3

There was no alternative: mother had two children, and was in poor health; and so she decided that the three of us should enter the Lambeth workhouse. There we were made to separate. Mother went in one direction to the women's ward and we in another to the children's. I remember well the sadness of that first visiting day: the shock of seeing Mother enter the visiting-room dressed in workhouse clothes. How sad and embarrassed she looked.

Charles (Charlie) Chaplin

Activity 2

Look at Source 3.3. In your own words, explain why the experience of the workhouse was so upsetting. You should explain at least two pieces of evidence. (N4 British AS 1.1)

SOURCE 3.4

How would you feel if you had to spend all day doing the kind of work in Source 3.4?

These women are unpicking old rope, a common job in the workhouse. The fibres were then used to help make wooden ships watertight.

Richard Oastler, writing in 1841, studied the food on offer to an inmate of the poorhouse and concluded that the diet was worse than that available to prisoners in jail.

The Poor Law system made state help unattractive to many poor people. It has been estimated that 90 per cent of the unemployed never used poor relief even though they needed help.

Why was the Poor Law system so harsh?

Many people at the time believed that if you went to a workhouse you had obviously failed to look after yourself or your family properly. Asking for help at a workhouse was seen as a sign of a failure of character. If you could not look after yourself and your family, you must be either lazy or wasting too much money on drink and gambling. The poor were expected to look after themselves by saving money, living a sober life and working hard.

The government was also worried that if too much help was provided by the government for the poor, this would encourage the poor not to look for work. Living on government help would be seen as being easier than getting a job. This would become very expensive as more poor people would rely on government help rather than their own efforts to escape poverty.

Views such as Helen Bosanquet's were common in Britain:

SOURCE 3.5

To have classified a man as belonging to the poor means that we no longer expect from him the qualities of independence and responsibility which we assume as a matter of course in other people. We suppose he cannot be a good workman. We expect him to make no effort on his part to raise himself above poverty. We expect him to live in a slum and for him to have no intelligent interests or amusements. We think of him only as a drunken brute.

Helen Bosanquet, The Strength of the People (1902)

SOURCE 3.6

Why do you think the women in the workhouse might be embarrassed by having to live this way?

The inmates of a workhouse in London, England at the beginning of the twentieth century. Such 'paupers' were not considered to be proper human beings by many people.

Activity 3

Wordsearch

Draw a grid, ten squares by ten, large enough so that you can write letters in each of the boxes.

Use the wordsearch to hide at least five main words (ideas or names) linked to the problem with poverty.

Complete the grid with random letters to conceal your words. Do not show where the words are on your grid. Your partner must find them. Write definitions of the words below or beside your wordsearch.

When you have completed your wordsearch, exchange it with your partner. Read their clues and find the words. As they solve your puzzle, you solve theirs.

Activity 4

Summarise this chapter

Write a short summary of this chapter describing the old system of poor relief. You must describe the system of poor relief in both Scotland, and England and Wales in as few sentences as possible. Try to include an answer to the following question: 'What help was given to those in poverty before the Liberal welfare reforms?'

Activity 5

Freeze frame

Work in small groups as directed by your teacher. You are going to physically pose in a snapshot representation of life in a workhouse and show how it might look in a freeze frame.

The scenes you might choose to represent could be:

▶ going into a workhouse
▶ being separated from your family
▶ mealtimes in a workhouse
▶ being punished in a workhouse
▶ working in a workhouse
▶ dying in a workhouse.

Once you have chosen your workhouse scene, work together with your group to discuss what you are being asked to show and how it might look in a freeze frame.

Take it in turns to view other groups' freeze frames.

You might act out the developments in order, taking photos to create a photo-story with captions beneath each picture.

You could then have a class discussion afterwards about why each group decided to act out the scene in the way they did.

Chapter summary

▶ The government provided limited help to those who were very poor.
▶ This help was found in the workhouse in England/Wales and the poorhouse in Scotland.
▶ Conditions in the workhouse were deliberately harsh to stop people seeking help.
▶ Those that sought help were thought to suffer from some personal failing.
▶ In reality the Poor Law could not cope with the scale of poverty.

Question practice

NATIONAL 4

Source A is about conditions in the workhouse:

SOURCE A

Discipline was strictly enforced. For minor offences such as swearing or pretending to be sick the 'disorderly' inmate could have their diet restricted for up to 48 hours.

Life in a workhouse was intended to be harsh, to deter the **able-bodied** *poor and to ensure that only the truly destitute would apply.*

> **GLOSSARY**
> **Able-bodied** fit and healthy

1 **Describe the ways in which life in the workhouse could be unpleasant. You should use Source A in your answer.** (N4 British 2.1)

Success criteria

Include at least two points of information, or one point of information that is fully explained, about the ways in which life in the workhouse could be unpleasant.

NATIONAL 5

1 Describe the Poor Law system before 1906. (6 marks)

You would not get a source to help with this question in the exam, but use the following prompt card to help get you started:

Prompt card

- Indoor relief
- Outdoor relief
- Workhouse system in England and Wales
- Poorhouse system in Scotland
- No help for able-bodied poor
- Conditions in the workhouse/poorhouse

Success criteria

- Include six factual pieces of information on the Poor Law system before 1906.

OR

- Include at least three developed pieces of information on the Poor Law system before 1906.
- Give accurate and detailed pieces of information that are properly explained.

Source A is by a man called J.F. Oakeshott in 1894. Oakeshott was a Socialist who did not like the workhouse system.

SOURCE A

Many men and women every year deliberately prefer death by starvation outside the workhouse to accepting relief from the rates [the workhouse]. They do not want to lose their freedoms and do not want to be treated like prisoners. The old and the young, the sick and able-bodied, the deserving and undeserving alike do not want the **stigma***, or disgrace of being a pauper unable to look after themselves.*

GLOSSARY

Stigma a mark of disgrace or shame

2 How fully does Source A explain why people disliked going to the workhouse? (5 marks)

Success criteria

- Place the source in context by explaining information in the source and applying that information to your own knowledge.
- Up to three marks may be given for explaining pieces of information from the source.
- Up to four marks may be given for explaining pieces of information from your own knowledge which are relevant to the question asked.
- Pieces of information from your own knowledge can be used as further explanation of information from the source or as new points.

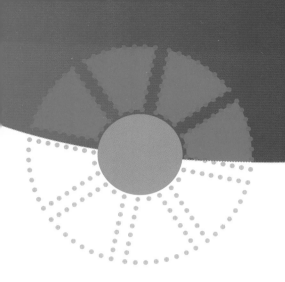

Chapter 4 What were the attitudes towards poverty before 1906?

What is this chapter about?

Attitudes to poverty were very different from today. Many believed in self-help; the idea that everyone should take personal responsibility for themselves and their families. There were many organisations set up, based on the idea of self-help, such as friendly societies and the co-operative movement. Charities also played a big role in helping the poor.

By the end of this chapter you should be able to:

▸ Explain what 'self-help' means.
▸ Describe the different organisations that encouraged self-help.

Many people believed self-help was the best way to avoid poverty. One of the most important people who believed in this was Samuel Smiles, born in Haddington, East Lothian in 1812. He qualified as a doctor from Edinburgh University. Today he is remembered for his writings. His most famous and important book, called *Self-Help* and published in 1859, was very popular.

Smiles believed that effort and positive thinking could make anything possible. This **maxim** helped create a spirit of industry and enterprise that encouraged people to improve themselves through hard work. Ideas led to inventions, which led to the making of fortunes. It was these ideas and inventions that had made Britain rich through the Industrial Revolution.

Smiles argued that:

GLOSSARY

Maxim a statement or saying that aims to sum up a general experience or idea

SOURCE 4.1

'Heaven helps those who help themselves' is a well tried saying, in which can be found all human experience. The spirit of self-help is the root of all genuine growth in the individual; and, in the lives of the many, it shows the true source of national strength and vigour.

Smiles warned against governments helping people too much. This help was bad because it made men helpless. He thought that the role of governments should be very limited. Smiles said:

SOURCE 4.2

Any help given to a man or class takes away the need of doing it for themselves. Where men are subjected to over-guidance and over government, the result is to leave them dependent. Every day it is becoming more clearly understood, that government is negative and restrictive, rather than positive and active. No laws, however severe, can make the idle work harder, the spenders careful with money, or the drunken sober. Poverty can only be escaped by means of individual action, economy, and self-denial; by better habits, rather than by greater rights.

This belief in self-help is important because it led many people in Britain to believe that poverty could be beaten by positive thinking and hard work alone. Smiles said that the average worker could avoid poverty by working hard and saving some of their wages. These savings could be used whenever the worker was out of a job, or became unable to work because of illness or old age.

Smiles thought that there was no need for the government to become involved in providing for the poor. It was the duty of people to look after themselves. Those that did not were either idle, unable or unwilling to save, or drunks.

What self-help was there?

Self-help worked for those members of the working class who had a regular income, large enough to allow savings to be made. These workers tended to be skilled. There were many places where they could save money to provide for illness, unemployment and old age.

Friendly Societies

Friendly Societies were the most popular way in which people helped themselves. Benefits were given out based on the contributions an individual made. J. Tidd Pratt, in his book, *Suggestions for the Establishment of Friendly Societies* (1855), summed up the ideas behind Friendly Societies:

> **GLOSSARY**
> **Friendly Society** a partnership association for the purposes of insurance, pensions, savings or banking

SOURCE 4.3

*Friendly Societies are formed on the principle of **mutual** insurance. Each member contributes a certain sum by weekly or monthly subscriptions while he is in health, for which he expects to receive from the society a certain provision or allowance when he is incapacitated for work by accident, sickness, or old age.*

J. Tidd Pratt, Suggestions for the Establishment of Friendly Societies (1855)

> **GLOSSARY**
> **Mutual** a partnership with others for joint benefit

By the 1890s it was estimated that 8 million people had made some sort of contribution to a Friendly Society. Most Friendly Societies also ran social activities, such as an annual parade or gala day.

Savings banks

Savings banks were very popular with servants and those who were saving for their children. There were even 'penny savings banks', which were aimed at the very poor, who could only save very small amounts of money. The increasing numbers who used these banks during the nineteenth century was a good sign, according to some. Savings meant people had money at times of difficulty. It also encouraged good habits such as saving and living within a budget.

The Post Office also opened savings accounts. These were extremely popular, with 663,000 opening accounts between 1863 and 1868. They grew to 5,776,000 by the 1890s.

The Co-operative Movement

SOURCE 4.4

How would a shop like this benefit the local community?

The Falkland Equitable Co-operative Society, circa 1890

Members of the working class helped themselves by forming Co-operative Societies. This involved a community getting together to provide low cost food and services for themselves. For example, a grocery store or a funeral parlour.

Not everyone liked the idea of self-help. Those who were critical of self-help pointed out that not all people could save for a 'rainy day'. Lack of education and poor health also stopped many people improving their lives. It was not possible for everybody to improve their life by positive thinking alone.

What was the role of charities in helping the poor?

The Poor Law only gave help for the very poor. Further help came from the many charities that were founded during the nineteenth century. Work done by charities included:

▶ giving money to the poor
▶ giving time to help the poor
▶ providing some particular expertise to help the poor.

Many of these charities, such as the RSPCA, Dr Barnado's and the Salvation Army continue to exist today. There were a huge number of charities. One survey of London in 1861 identified no fewer than 640 charitable organisations helping the poor. This help ranged from hospitals for the ill and orphanages, to Bible missionary activities. Private charity in the eighteenth and nineteenth centuries was far more important than the Poor Law in the day-to-day relief of poverty.

In Scotland, charities were even more important as the official Poor Law only gave help to a very small group of the poor. The only groups to get help would be the old, the young and the disabled. The 1897 report of the Annual Conference of the Charity Organisation Society stated that Glasgow charities raised £1 million per year while the Edinburgh charities raised £250,000 per year.

Most charities providing help for the poor were frequently organised by well-meaning middle-class men and women. These people had a number of reasons for running charities:

SOURCE 4.5

Octavia Hill (1838–1912)

▶ Fear that the poor would rise up against those wealthier than themselves in revolution. Charity would stop this.
▶ Genuine concern. Many charities were motivated by Christian concern for the plight of their fellow man and woman.
▶ It was an opportunity for middle-class women to get involved in public life. By 1900, more jobs were opening up to women but charities remained an area where women could organise and make a real difference.
▶ The desire to help the poor lead a 'better' life.
▶ Most people who ran charities were strong believers in the ideas of Samuel Smiles. They did not think poverty was the result of circumstances outwith the poor's control such as unemployment. Most believed that poverty was caused by the poor having some personal failing.

GLOSSARY

Squalor extremely poor living conditions

A typical example of the well-meaning individual who provided charity was that of Octavia Hill (1838–1912). Octavia Hill was a middle-class lady who was interested in the link between poverty and bad housing. She believed that slums were created because landlords did not care about maintaining their properties. Octavia Hill also thought that tenants in these properties helped create these slums by their bad behaviour and willingness to live in **squalor**. Hill tried to change this by managing property in a better way. She made sure that the properties she managed were well maintained. In return, she expected her tenants to pay their rent on time and to live respectable and responsible lives. Octavia Hill thought that charitable help should include education of the poor in how to lead better lives as well as practical help. She thought that this educational work was best done by people like herself. Octavia Hill was totally against government help for the poor.

Hill's ideas were very common among those who provided charity. They felt that they were responsible for improving the way the poor led their lives. People such as Hill tended to be members of the Charity Organisation Society (COS), which was founded in 1869. The COS felt that the type of help given should relate to the particular circumstances of the person seeking help. They also thought that charity must do more than simply give help; the help must have a purpose.

SOURCE 4.6

What do you think the aims of the farm colonies were?

A Salvation Army poster advertises William Booth's farm colonies in Essex and Hertfordshire. These farms were where those who had been saved from the misery of the cities would find a new life.

There were other reasons for starting charities. Many charity leaders were religious. One of the most famous individuals was William Booth (1829–1919).

In 1861, William Booth started the Salvation Army. To begin with he hoped to save souls by converting the poor to God. But he came to believe that his religious campaign would never be successful unless poverty was ended. He hoped to achieve this by setting up work colonies where the poor could be retrained and live more productive lives. Again, Booth hoped to improve the poor through retraining and religious education in the Christian faith. As Booth said:

SOURCE 4.7

To save a man properly it is not enough to put on him a pair of new trousers, to give him regular work, or even to give him a University education. These things are all outside a man, and if the inside remains unchanged you have wasted your effort.

William Booth

Despite the beliefs of charity leaders, the existence of so many charities was evidence that not everybody who was poor could improve themselves and escape poverty. Few people were willing to admit to this. However, the attitudes behind charity were soon to be challenged by research that would show that poverty had complicated and varied causes. It was by no means clear that the cause of poverty was the fault of the person who was poor.

Chapter summary

- Self-help meant that people could escape poverty by saving money and living a sensible life. Such ideas were very popular in this period.
- The working class were encouraged to save through organisations like Friendly Societies and Savings Banks.
- The working class helped themselves by setting up Co-operative stores to provide good food at a fair price.
- Not everybody believed that all poor people could save money for a 'rainy day'.
- Charities were very important in helping those who were poor.
- Charitable help was given for a number of reasons.
- Charity sought to help people by improving the way in which they led their lives.

Activity 1

If this is the answer, what is the question?

Below you will find a list of words or names. You have to make up a question that can only be answered by the words on the list. For example, if the name 'Octavia Hill' was the answer, a question could be 'What was the name of a well-known charity provider in London?' Write the question and answer in your work file.

- self-help
- Samuel Smiles
- Friendly Societies
- Co-operative movement
- William Booth
- Salvation Army

Activity 2

Summarise this chapter

Take a whole page in your workbook or work file. Add the title: 'Self-help and charities'.

Now draw up a table with four columns headed: 'Self-help', 'Friendly Societies', 'Savings Banks and the Co-operative Movement', and 'Charitable help'. In each column, list the names of key ideas, people and organisations that relate to helping the poor before 1906.

Now, write a short paragraph answering the following question: 'What help was given to the poor before 1906?' Support your answer with evidence from the table you have drawn up.

Question practice

NATIONAL 4

Source A is about why charities tried to change the way people led their lives.

SOURCE A

It is more important to develop self-respect and good judgement than just to meet physical needs. If you are able to change the way a man lives his life, then your money will have had a permanent effect on his life.

1 **Explain why many charities tried to change the way the poor led their lives. You can use Source A or your own knowledge.** (N4 British AS 2.2)

Success criteria

You must explain at least one point showing why charities tried to change the way the poor led their lives.

Source B is about Octavia Hill:

SOURCE B

Octavia Hill was a social reformer who worked mainly in London. She spent most of her time trying to improve housing for poor people. Octavia Hill even built her own tenements for respectable working poor to live in.

2 **Look at Source B. Describe the charity work done by Octavia Hill. You should make at least two points.** (N4 British AS 2.1)

Success criteria

You should make at least two relevant, factual points of information or a single point which is well developed about the charity work done by Octavia Hill.

NATIONAL 5

Source A is by a modern historian, Rosemary Rees, written in 2001:

SOURCE A

The effort which the poor were supposed to put into helping themselves out of poverty was called 'Self-Help'. Everyone, no matter how poor, could raise themselves and their families to a well-off position. There was no need for the rich to pay high taxes to pay for the poor because showing concern for your neighbours meant giving them the chance to practise 'self-help' too. Only a small number of genuinely needy people required help.

1   Evaluate the usefulness of Source A as evidence of the ideas of self-help on poverty. (6 marks)

Success criteria

▶ For a mark to be given, you must identify an aspect of the source and make a comment which shows how this aspect makes the source more or less useful.
▶ Up to four marks may be given for points about **author**, **type of source**, **purpose** and **timing**.
▶ Up to two marks may be given for your evaluation of which content within the source you consider to be useful in terms of the proposed question. For full marks to be given each point needs to be discretely mentioned and its usefulness explained.
▶ If you list information, that will be considered to be one point and will get only one mark.
▶ Up to two marks may be given for the application of relevant and developed pieces of recalled information. This has to be relevant to the question for full marks to be given.

2   Describe the reasons why so many middle- and upper-class people became involved in providing charity for the poor. (5 marks)

You would not get a source to help with this question in the exam, but use the following prompt card to help get you started:

Prompt card

▶ Belief in self-help
▶ Fear that the poor would rebel against the well-off
▶ Genuine concern
▶ Information from social investigators
▶ A chance for middle-class women to get involved in public life
▶ The desire to help the poor lead a 'better' life
▶ Religious beliefs.

Success criteria

▶ Include five factual pieces of information on why people got involved in providing charity.
OR
▶ Include at least three developed pieces of information on why people got involved in providing charity.
▶ Give accurate and detailed pieces of information that are properly explained.

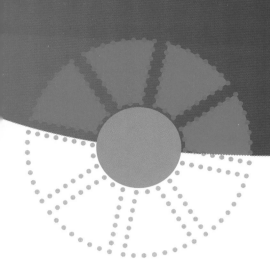

Chapter 5 Why did the surveys of Booth and Rowntree cause changes in attitudes to poverty?

What is this chapter about?

By the end of the nineteenth century, the old system of poor relief was not fit for purpose. However, not everyone was convinced that the system should change. Social investigators set out to find out how much hardship there really was – and what caused it. Two men were very important in this process: Charles Booth and Seebohm Rowntree. Together, their work created a new understanding of poverty and changed attitudes on what help should be given to the poor.

By the end of this chapter, you should be able to:

▶ Explain who Charles Booth was.
▶ Explain who Seebohm Rowntree was.
▶ Describe what they found out about poverty in the surveys they carried out.
▶ Explain why these surveys were so important.

Charles Booth and Seebohm Rowntree were both wealthy men who studied poverty, its causes and its effects. They became well known as a result of the work they did studying poverty in Britain.

The books of people like Andrew Mearns (see Chapter 2) had shocked wealthy Victorians. Charles Booth was one such man. He was originally a Liverpool ship owner. At first he believed that the level of poverty in Britain was limited and could be dealt with by charity. In common with most people of his class, he thought that if people were poor it was their own fault.

SOURCE 5.1

Charles Booth, 1840–1916

Booth wanted to know how much hardship there really was in Britain. Between 1889 and 1903 he studied the life of the poor in London, publishing his findings in 17 volumes as *Life and Labour of the People in London*. His findings changed his opinion about the levels of poverty in London. Booth concluded that 30 per cent of London's population was living in poverty. Booth's work was important for a number of reasons:

▶ His method of working was important. He used scientific methods and put people into recognisable social classes.
▶ He worked out a 'poverty line' (a level of income that was needed in order for a family to stay just beyond a life of starvation).
▶ He provided statistics that showed how widespread poverty was.
▶ The scale of the poverty he uncovered could not be met by charitable aid alone.

With a partner, calculate the percentage of people living in London who were classed as poor.

SOURCE 5.2

	Population classification
A	The lowest class – wasters and semi-criminals.
B	The very poor – casual labour, hand-to-mouth existence.
C and D	The poor – including those whose earnings are small, because of irregular employment, and those whose work is low paid.
E and F	The regularly employed and fairly paid working class of all grades.
G and H	Lower and upper middle class and all above these levels.

SOURCE 5.3

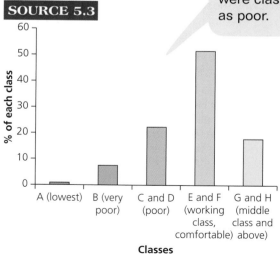

Booth's findings were supported by another social investigator called Seebohm
Rowntree. Rowntree was a member of a wealthy chocolate manufacturing family
from York. After reading about Booth's work on poverty in London, Rowntree
decided to see if the level of poverty in York was different to that in London. In
1901 he published his book, *Poverty: A Study of Town Life*. His findings were similar
to those of Booth.

SOURCE 5.4

Seebohm Rowntree, 1871–1954

Rowntree was important because:

- He showed that poverty was not just a problem in London. The York study
  proved that poverty was widespread. One third of the population living in towns
  lived in poverty.
- His study was also important because of the methods he used to carry out his
  study. Rowntree identified two types of poverty. Primary poverty was used to
  describe those people whose earnings were so low they could not survive on
  them alone. Secondary poverty was used to describe those whose earnings
  were enough to live on but who spent money in a wasteful way.
- He fixed a 'poverty line' (a figure on the amount of money a worker needed to
  earn in order to maintain a family in a minimum standard of living).

SOURCE 5.5

*The average weekly wage for a labourer in York is from 18s. to 21s. but the minimum
expenditure necessary to maintain a family of two adults and three children is 21s. 8d. or,
if there are four children, the sum required would be 26s.*

From B.S. Rowntree, Poverty: A Study of Town Life (1901)

Activity 1

Explain, in your own words, why wages were too low for a labourer living in York. You should give two pieces of information in your answer. (N4 British AS 1.1/2.1)

SOURCE 5.6

Let us clearly understand how a family lives if they are on the minimum income required. A family must never spend a penny on railway fare or bus. They must never buy a halfpenny newspaper or spend a penny to buy a ticket for a popular concert. They can't send letters to absent children, because they cannot afford to buy stamps. They can't give money to their church or chapel, or give any help to a neighbour which costs them money. They are not able to save, nor can they join the sick club or trade union, because they cannot pay the necessary subscriptions. The children will get no pocket money for treats. The father mustn't smoke or drink beer. The mother must never buy any pretty clothes for herself or for her children. [...] The family cannot afford to pay any medical or funeral costs. Finally, the wage-earner must never be absent from his work for a single day.

From B.S. Rowntree, Poverty: A Study of Town Life *(1901)*

Activity 2

Explain, in your own words, how a family lived who were on the minimum income required. You should give at least three pieces of information in your answer. (N5 British AS 1.1/2.1)

These investigators of social conditions found that poverty was not always the fault of the person who was poor. Many of the elderly, the ill and those without work lived poor lives. However, many workers were paid wages so low, or were not paid regularly due to irregular work, that they could not afford life's basic needs. The poverty of these people was not their fault.

How important were Booth and Rowntree?

Booth and Rowntree were not professional researchers but they changed the way poverty was studied. They were very important men. Historians agree:

SOURCE 5.7

The social surveys did tend to undermine the view that personal character defects were the primary cause of poverty.

From J.R. Hay, The Origins of the Liberal Welfare Reforms *(1975)*

SOURCE 5.8

Booth and Rowntree gave to the growing public concern over poverty the statistical evidence on which to build the case for state aid.

From D. Fraser, The Evolution of the British Welfare State (1984)

Chapter summary

▶ Charles Booth and Seebohm Rowntree were private individuals who studied the amount of poverty in London and York.
▶ They brought new methods to study the amount of poverty that existed.
▶ Their findings showed that approximately 30 per cent of the urban population in Britain was living in poverty. This was the first time the scale of poverty had been calculated.
▶ Their findings showed that the amount of poverty that existed required levels of help that could only be provided by the British Government. Charity was not enough.

Activity 3

Creating a fishbone diagram

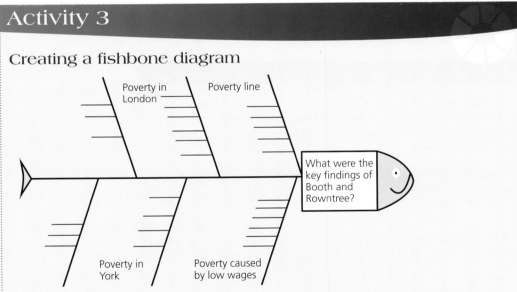

Copy the artwork onto an A4 sheet of paper (or bigger, if you like!) and write the following question at the tip, or nose, of the skeleton: 'What were the key findings of Booth and Rowntree?'

Write the answers to the question on your diagram, with the main findings running along the main fish bones. Write along the smaller horizontal bones to add in further detail about the main findings. Some have been filled in for you already.

Your main findings should include:

▶ causes of poverty
▶ primary poverty
▶ secondary poverty.

Activity 4

The challenge! How far can you go?

The following questions go up in level of difficulty in pairs. The first two are easy. The last two are hard. How many will you try to do?

1 Name two important social investigators.
2 Name the two cities where the social investigators did their research.
3 Describe what was discovered about poverty in London.
4 Describe what was discovered about poverty in York.
5 Explain why Booth and Rowntree were important in changing attitudes to poverty.
6 'The most important impact of Booth and Rowntree was in providing evidence of poverty in London and York.' Do you agree or disagree with this statement? You will need to be able to support your answer with evidence.

Question practice

NATIONAL 4

Source A was written by historian Theo Barker:

SOURCE A

Poverty began to attract more attention because concerned men like the ship owner Charles Booth and the chocolate manufacturer Seebohm Rowntree, began to investigate it. They revealed the real causes of poverty for the first time. They also showed how big the problem was.

1 **Look at Source A. Explain why Charles Booth and Seebohm Rowntree's findings on poverty were important.** (N4 British 2.2)

Success criteria

You must explain at least one point showing why Booth and Rowntree's findings were important.

NATIONAL 5

Sources A and B are about Booth and Rowntree's findings on the reasons for poverty.

SOURCE A

Booth showed that poverty was caused by circumstances as much as the fault of the individual. Most poverty was caused by problems with employment. Booth highlighted the problem of only finding work at certain times of the year. Low wages were another cause of poverty because no matter how hard someone worked, they didn't have enough to live on. Old age was another big cause of poverty as the elderly had no income when they were no longer able to work.

SOURCE B

Rowntree's research helped understanding of the reasons for poverty. Rowntree showed that 10 per cent of the population still lived in poverty no matter what they did. He also showed that low wages were beyond the control of the individual and caused much poverty. Old age was another key cause because at a certain point in someone's life, they couldn't work. Illness was as important as old age, especially of the main wage earner, because it meant the family lacked a regular income.

1 Compare the views of Sources A and B about the reasons for poverty before 1906. (4 marks)

Success criteria

▶ You should interpret evidence from the sources.
▶ Make direct comparisons between the information in the sources.
▶ Up to two marks may be given for comparing how far the two sources agree or disagree overall.
▶ Up to four marks may be given for making direct comparisons between the information in the two sources.
▶ 'Source A says … and Source B agrees …' will get one mark. A developed comparison: 'Sources A and B agree on low wages causing poverty. Source A says … and Source B agrees, saying …' will get two marks.

Chapter 6 Why did concerns about the Empire cause changes in attitudes to poverty?

What is this chapter about?

People in Britain were worried about the future of the British Empire. They worried that other countries might challenge Britain for control over its Empire. In 1899, a war broke out in South Africa, which took Britain three long years to win. Britain was shocked by this and by the number of men who had been rejected for the British army because they were unfit. Many people argued that social reforms should be introduced to ensure a fit workforce and army to maintain Britain's power.

By the end of this chapter you should be able to:

▶ Explain why the Boer War worried people in Britain.
▶ Describe what National Efficiency means.
▶ Explain the impact of the Committee on Physical Deterioration.

In 1899 war broke out between the British and the **Boers** in South Africa. The British thought that the war would be over quickly. However, Boer fighters were well trained, equipped and led, and the war dragged on for three years. Eventually, Britain had to use 400,000 troops to defeat Boer forces that totalled just 35,000. The war was a great shock to British confidence. People searched for answers as to why it had taken three years for professional soldiers to defeat a force of Boer farmers.

> **GLOSSARY**
>
> **Boers** farmers in South Africa descended from Dutch settlers

SOURCE 6.1

Wounded British soldiers outside a hospital during the Boer War.

Activity 1

I see, I think, I wonder…

In pairs, think about how this picture would have affected public opinion in Britain.

The poor quality of soldiers was blamed for how Britain did in the war. In some towns, as many as nine out of ten recruits for the army were rejected because they were so unfit. In Source 6.2 Arnold White speaks about the numbers of recruits rejected in Manchester:

SOURCE 6.2

In Manchester 11,000 men volunteered between the outbreak of war in October 1899 and July 1900. Of this number 8000 were found to be physically unfit to carry a rifle and cope with army life. Of the 3000 who were accepted, only 1200 met the standard of fighting fitness required by the military. In other words, two out of every three men willing to fight in the Manchester district are virtually invalids.

Arnold White, Efficiency and Empire (1901)

Activity 2

Look at Source 6.2. Explain why so many volunteers were rejected by the army in Manchester. You should make at least two points. (N5 British AS 2.2)

After the war, Major-General Sir Frederick Maurice in an article entitled, *National Health: A Soldier's Study*, complained about another problem:

SOURCE 6.3

... out of every five men who volunteer, you will find that by the end of two years' service there are only two men remaining in the Army as effective soldiers.

Major-General Sir Frederick Maurice, National Health: A Soldier's Study (1903)

Activity 3

Look at Source 6.3. Explain the army's problem with volunteers at the time of the Boer War. You should explain one point of information. (N4 British AS 2.2)

The dropout rate for volunteers was very worrying for a country like Britain trying to run a large Empire. It implied that not only were men unfit, but they were unwilling to work as well. Some people thought they had found an explanation for why the British army had performed so badly in South Africa – and why other countries were overtaking Britain in economic growth.

Arnold White and others blamed the poor living conditions in Britain's towns:

SOURCE 6.4

*Population growth in towns has been created by industrialisation. Most of this population is unable to fight. Weak, hungry schoolchildren grow into adults with diseases like **tuberculosis**.*

Arnold White, Efficiency and Empire (1901)

GLOSSARY

Tuberculosis an infectious bacterial lung disease

Importantly, the Boer War was even further evidence that Britain was not doing enough to help the poorest in society.

SOURCE 6.5

The high number of army volunteers from the large towns rejected as physically unfit appeared to confirm the alarming findings of Booth and Rowntree.

A. Sykes, The Rise and Fall of British Liberalism (1997)

People like Arnold White argued that the Boer War and poor British economic performance (see Chapter 2) were proof of British decline. Their views were very common at this time. One response to this problem was to argue for social reforms that would create a healthy population. In turn, this would lead to a more efficient workforce and army. This argument was called 'National Efficiency'.

One of the results of the Boer War was the setting up in 1903 of a specially appointed Committee on Physical **Deterioration** to find out why so many army recruits had been rejected. The Committee reported in 1904 that they had found no evidence of long-term physical ill health in the population in Britain. They made many recommendations, including medical inspection of children in schools, free school meals for the very poor and training in mothering skills.

> **GLOSSARY**
> **Deterioration** to get worse

The findings of the Committee were very important in shaping future Liberal reforms. According to historian Eric Evans, the importance of the Boer War was huge:

SOURCE 6.6

Arguably, the single most important reason for causing the social reforms between 1905 and 1914 was fear of the consequences of an unfit population.

Eric Evans

Chapter summary

▶ The Boer War seemed to show that the population of Britain was unfit and unhealthy.
▶ The number of unfit and unhealthy men was blamed for the 'decline' of the British Empire.
▶ In order for Britain's population to become more 'efficient', social reforms were proposed.

Activity 4

Summarise this chapter

The following summary reminds you of what this chapter has been about. Words that are important have been made into ANAGRAMS. Your task is to sort out the anagrams and then write the correct version of this summary into your workbook or work file.

The **BROW ARE** lasted for three years, from 1899 to 1902. People in Britain were shocked at how long it took for a professional army to defeat **FARMRES.** They were even more shocked at the large number of **NERVOUSLET** who were rejected because they were **PAINFULLY SHY TIC**. Britons began to worry that they would not be able to maintain her **MEPIER** if troops were so unfit. An important government committee was set up to decide what should be done. They decided that Britain had to become more **FENCEIFIT** and recommended that **FIREARMS COOLS** be made to help poor people. Many of their suggestions were aimed at helping the **GOUYN**. Some historians think that the most important reason for the **FORMS BILLER** was fear of the effect of **VERYTOP** on Britain's **HAWLET**.

Activity 5

Question expert

Your teacher will divide you into small groups to make up a quiz about how concerns about Empire helped cause the social reforms.

1 Each group will be given three different coloured Post-it notes.
2 Each group must make up three questions about how concerns about the Empire helped cause social reform. One question ('green') should be easy; one question ('amber') quite hard; one question ('red') really hard. The group should make a note of the expected answer for each question in their workbooks or work files. Write the questions on the Post-its and put the group name/number on the back.
3 Stick the Post-it notes on the classroom wall or whiteboard as directed by the teacher.
4 The teacher will then run a class quiz with a series of rounds. In each round, one member of the group will choose one of the green, amber and red questions. They will take the question back to their group and write the answers in their workbook or work file. Once the group have answered the question, they will return the Post-it note to the board. Each member of the group must choose at least two questions during the quiz.
5 Each question level will have a mark attached to it. For example, green = 1 mark; amber = 2 marks; red = 3 marks.
6 At the end of the quiz, the teacher will check the answers to the questions with the 'question expert'. The winner is the team with the most number of points.

Question practice

NATIONAL 4

SOURCE A

Many volunteers were unable to hold a rifle and march in line. They had to be rejected. Others were accepted by the army, but were not classed as fighting fit and could only take on support roles. Three out of every five volunteers dropped out of the army after two years.

1 **Describe the problems Britain had in recruiting volunteers for the Boer War.**
(N4 British AS 2.1)

Success criteria

You should describe at least two pieces of evidence about the problems Britain had recruiting.

NATIONAL 5

1 Explain the reasons why concerns about the British Empire led to the Liberal welfare reforms. (6 marks)

This is an 'explain' question. This means you must give six reasons why something did or did not happen. It is not enough to just write down facts, no matter how correct they are. You must link each fact back to the question, explaining how that fact did or did not allow something to happen. For this question, this means you need to explain why the concerns about the Empire helped cause the Liberal reforms.

To get you started on your answer, here are some hints:

▶ Explain why the length of the Boer War worried people in Britain, leading to the Liberal reforms.
▶ Explain why the number of unfit volunteers for the war worried people in Britain, leading to the Liberal reforms.
▶ Explain why the dropout rate of army volunteers worried people in Britain, leading to the Liberal reforms.
▶ Explain how the Boer War confirmed the findings of social investigators, leading to the Liberal reforms.
▶ Explain why the report from the Committee on Physical Deterioration helped lead to the Liberal reforms.

Success criteria

▶ Include six factual pieces of information on why concerns led to the Liberal welfare reforms.

OR

▶ Include at least three developed pieces of information on why concerns led to the Liberal welfare reforms.
▶ Give accurate and detailed pieces of information that are properly explained.

SOURCE A

Concerns were expressed about the 'national efficiency' of the British people. The Boer War seemed to confirm a decline in Britain's fighting strength. Britain had taken a long time to defeat an inferior enemy. Recruitment centres found high numbers of the volunteers were rejected on grounds of being physically unfit. One general claimed that only two out of every five soldiers were still fit for service after two years. This he claimed, reflected the general level of unfitness of the British people.

2 How fully does Source A explain why the Boer War led to the Liberal reforms? (5 marks)

Success criteria

▶ Place the source in context by explaining information in the source and applying that information to your own knowledge.
▶ Up to two marks may be given if only the source or recall is given.
▶ Up to three marks may be given for explaining pieces of information from the source.
▶ Up to four marks may be given for explaining pieces of information from your own knowledge which are relevant to the question asked.
▶ Pieces of information from your own knowledge can be used as further explanation of information in the source or as new points.

Chapter 7 Why did political changes help cause the Liberal reforms?

What is this chapter about?

By the twentieth century, most men were able to vote in elections. This helped cause social reforms because more working-class people could vote and government had to pass reforms that met their needs. This growth in democracy also changed the political parties in Britain. The Labour Party was created leading to more demands for reform. The Liberal Party also changed their ideas and became more keen to introduce social reform.

By the end of this chapter you should be able to:

- Explain why political parties had to think more about passing social reforms by the start of the twentieth century.
- Explain why working-class voters supported the Labour Party.
- Explain why the Liberal Party wanted to introduce social reform.
- Explain the roles of Lloyd George and Winston Churchill.

Why did democratic change help lead to social reform?

After the 1884 Reform Act, six out of every ten men could now vote in elections. This meant that by 1905, most working men were able to vote. Working-class voters could now elect people who wanted to change the way Britain was run, and any government that wanted to get elected would have to respond to working-class concerns.

How did the trade union movement help lead to social reform?

In the 1890s, membership of trade unions grew from 1.6 million to just over 2 million members. Unions now represented not only skilled craft workers, but also unskilled and semi-skilled workers. In the 1890s there were several big strikes. Employers used the law to punish trade unions by making them pay the cost of the strikes. Trade unions were frustrated that the Liberals and the Conservatives didn't seem able to help them so they gave their support for a new Labour Party. The trade union movement hoped that the Labour party would do more to help ordinary working-class people. This put pressure on the Liberals and Conservatives to develop their own social reforms if they wanted to keep the votes of the working class.

SOURCE 7.1

What social problem is this poster drawing attention to?

A Labour Party election poster from the 1910 elections.

How did the spread of socialism help lead to reform?

In the late nineteenth century, **socialism** became a very popular idea. Many socialists felt very strongly that the government should do more to deal with poverty in Britain. The young Labour Party supported socialism.

The Labour Party started to grow slowly. Working-class voters had traditionally voted for the Liberal Party. They continued to do so for some time.

GLOSSARY

Socialism the idea that the resources and wealth of a country should be shared among its people

SOURCE 7.2

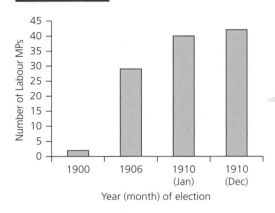

General election results for Labour, 1900–10

Labour's election manifesto from 1906 appealed for practical action to attack poverty:

SOURCE 7.3

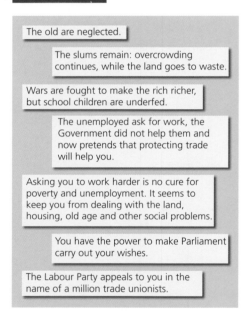

The old are neglected.

The slums remain: overcrowding continues, while the land goes to waste.

Wars are fought to make the rich richer, but school children are underfed.

The unemployed ask for work, the Government did not help them and now pretends that protecting trade will help you.

Asking you to work harder is no cure for poverty and unemployment. It seems to keep you from dealing with the land, housing, old age and other social problems.

You have the power to make Parliament carry out your wishes.

The Labour Party appeals to you in the name of a million trade unionists.

Labour election manifesto (1906)

Activity 1

Work with a partner. In your workbook or work file, create a mind map of the social problems Labour wanted to attack. You should use only pictures to express your ideas. You should note down at least three social problems. (N5 British 2.1)

The growth of the Labour Party pressurised the Liberal Party by threatening to take away the support Liberals had among working-class voters. This encouraged the Liberal Party to think hard about social reform.

Why did changes in Liberal ideas lead to reform?

Traditionally, Liberals had supported the ideas of self-help and minimal government action in people's lives. However, by the 1900s some Liberals were thinking that self-help had failed. These Liberals were called 'New Liberals'. They argued that the government should become involved in helping people.

Who were the Liberal Government?

In 1906 a General Election gave the Liberal Party a huge majority in Parliament:

SOURCE 7.4

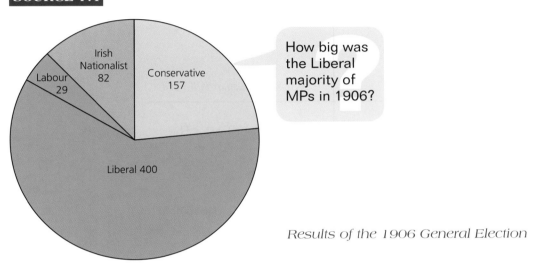

How big was the Liberal majority of MPs in 1906?

Results of the 1906 General Election

The Liberal Government was led by Henry Campbell-Bannerman until his death in 1908. Then Herbert Asquith took over as Prime Minister. The two most important New Liberals in the government were Winston Churchill and David Lloyd George. These politicians were willing to use the power of the government to intervene in society and try to end poverty. They did this for a number of reasons.

Factfile

Winston Churchill (1874–1965) is best remembered as a leader during the Second World War. He had a varied career before this. Churchill was a war journalist during the Boer War. In 1900, Churchill was elected as a Conservative MP. In 1904 he joined the Liberal Party after reading Rowntree's study of poverty in York. He became very interested in social reform as a result. In 1908 Churchill became President of the Board of Trade. In this job he achieved important social reforms such as the opening of **labour exchanges**. Churchill became Home Secretary in 1910, then First Lord of the Admiralty in 1911. In 1922 he rejoined the Conservative Party and in 1940 became Prime Minister.

GLOSSARY

Labour exchanges job centres

After reading Rowntree's study of poverty, Churchill said:

SOURCE 7.5

I see little glory in an Empire which can rule the waves, but is unable to clean its sewers.

Winston Churchill

Churchill had a genuine concern for the poor and the conditions in which they lived. In a speech at St Andrew's Hall, Glasgow, 11 October 1906, he said:

SOURCE 7.6

The cause of the Liberal Party is the cause of the left-out millions.

Winston Churchill (1906)

Churchill also saw social reform as a way of undermining the Labour Party. The historian A. Sykes has said:

SOURCE 7.7

Churchill thought that social reform was not only desirable in itself, but would also help support for the Liberal Party.

A. Sykes, The Rise and Fall of British Liberalism (1997)

Activity 2

Explain, in your own words, why Churchill wanted reforms. You should explain at least three different pieces of evidence. (N5 British 1.1/2.1)

Activity 3

Using your answer from Activity 2, group your evidence under headings why Churchill wanted reforms. Make a judgement on what you think was the most important reason Churchill wanted reform. (N5 British AS 1.2/2.3)

Factfile

David Lloyd George (1863–1945) was born in Manchester but was brought up in North Wales by his uncle, Richard Lloyd. In 1890 he was elected as Liberal MP of Caernarvon, North Wales. He was a brilliant public speaker. He was president of the Board of Trade (1905–08) then Chancellor of the Exchequer (1908–15). His own father had died due to ill health. He was committed to social reform and was very important in bringing in Old Age Pensions and the National Insurance Act. Lloyd George led the battle against the House of Lords to get the money to pay for the reforms. Lloyd George was Prime Minister between 1916 and 1922.

SOURCE 7.9

After all, this is a rich country. It is the richest country under the sun; and yet in this rich country you have hundreds and thousands of people living in such poverty that it would, in the words of an old Welsh poet, make the rocks weep.

Lloyd George's speech at Manchester (1908)

Churchill and Lloyd George were very important in leading the Liberal reforms. At the time they were seen as being very enthusiastic politicians. Maybe they were a little too enthusiastic according to the following cartoon.

SOURCE 7.10

"SUPPORTERS" RAMPANT.

AN HERALDIC INVERSION.

SOURCE 7.8

Lloyd George as a young man

Cartoon showing Asquith, the Prime Minister, balancing his two enthusiastic ministers on his shoulders. The cartoonist thinks that Asquith was embarrassed by the speeches of Lloyd George and Winston Churchill.

Chapter summary

▶ The Liberal Government was elected with a large majority in 1906.
▶ The Liberal Government had 'New' Liberals who were very interested in social reform.
▶ The two important government ministers who were especially interested in social reform were Winston Churchill and David Lloyd George.
▶ By the 1890s the increased number of working-class voters and their concerns led to the emergence of the Labour Party.
▶ The Labour Party stood for policies that appealed to working-class voters. Reform to deal with poverty was important to them.
▶ The Liberal Party also began to argue that the state had a role to play in dealing with the problems of society.

Activity 4

Topic triangle

This task is intended to help you summarise the contents of this chapter.

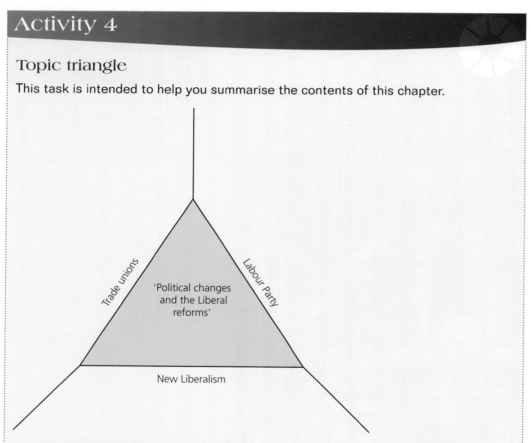

1 Take a whole page in your workbook or work file.
2 Draw a small triangle in the middle of your page, then divide the page into three. Look at the template for advice on how to do this.
3 In the middle of the small triangle, put the heading: 'Political changes and the Liberal reforms'.
4 On the sides of the triangle, put the headings: 'Trade unions', 'Labour Party' and 'New Liberalism'.
5 Fill up the space around each side of the triangle with key points about how that topic led to social reform. You can use pictures, symbols or writing to make your key points.

Activity 5

As a journalist, you have been asked to investigate and report on how changes in politics helped lead to the Liberal reforms. Think about what sort of questions you might want to ask. To help get you started, here are some hints:

▶ What were the key changes in who could vote?
▶ How did the growth of trade unions help lead to social reform?
▶ What impact did the growth of the Labour Party have on causing the Liberal reforms?
▶ What was New Liberalism?

Write these questions down in your workbook or work file and then add at least one more to those provided. Find evidence to answer these questions and note your answers in your workbook or work file.

Now you can plan your article. Make notes and structure what you are going to write in your report. Write the first draft of your article.

Read through your work carefully and mark any mistakes you spot with a green pen, then correct your work before handing it back to your teacher.

Ensure that information which answers all of the questions can be found in your article. Your article should be well structured and organised.

Question practice

NATIONAL 4

Philip Snowden, a leading member of the Labour Party, called on voters in 1900 to:

SOURCE A

Come and join us to remove poverty. Come and join us to bring hope to you and all your family for better health and happiness. Come and join us to benefit everyone in your community.

1 **Describe how the Labour Party attracted support from working-class voters.**
(N4 British AS 2.1)

Success criteria

You should give at least two points of information in your own words.

NATIONAL 5

1 Explain the reasons why the Labour Party threatened the Liberal Party's support from working-class voters. (5 marks)

This is an 'explain' question. This means you must give five reasons why something did or did not happen. It is not enough to just write down facts no matter how correct they are. You must link each fact back to the question, explaining how that fact did or did not allow something to happen. For this question, this means you need to explain why the Labour Party threatened the Liberal Party's support from working-class voters.

To get you started on your answer, here are some hints:

▶ Explain why the trade union labour struggles helped win the Labour Party support from the Liberals.
▶ Explain how the growth of socialist ideas helped win the Labour Party support from the Liberals.
▶ Explain how the growth of the Labour Party helped win the Labour Party support from the Liberals.
▶ Explain how the Labour Party's ideas on action to tackle poverty helped win the Labour Party support from the Liberals.

Success criteria

▶ Include five factual pieces of information on why the Labour Party threatened Liberal Party support.

OR

▶ Include at least three developed pieces of information on why the Labour Party threatened Liberal Party support.
▶ Give accurate and detailed pieces of information that are properly explained.

Source A is about why people in the Liberal Party turned to the ideas of New Liberalism, from the book, *Liberation* (1911), by L.T. Hobhouse (academic and journalist).

Source A

In the early days of industrialisation, it was hoped that the average workman would be able to keep himself in good times, but to also save for sickness, unemployment, and old age. These hopes have been disappointed. Although the standard of living in England has progressively advanced throughout the nineteenth century, there appears no likelihood that the average working man will be able to provide for himself and family, in all eventualities.

2 Evaluate the usefulness of Source A as evidence of the reasons many in the Liberal Party turned to New Liberal ideas. (5 marks)

Success criteria

▶ For a mark to be given, you must identify an aspect of the source and make a comment which shows how this aspect makes the source more or less useful.
▶ Up to four marks may be given for points about **author**, **type of source**, **purpose** and **timing**.
▶ Up to two marks may be given for your evaluation of the content of the source which you consider are useful in terms of the proposed question. For full marks to be given each point needs to be discretely mentioned and its usefulness explained.
▶ If you list information, that will be considered to be one point and will get only one mark.

▶ Up to two marks may be given for the application of relevant and developed pieces of recalled information. This has to be relevant to the question for full marks to be awarded.

This following task is intended to help you practise the 8-mark question in the external exam.

3 To what extent was genuine concern for the poor the reason for changing attitudes to poverty before 1906? (8 marks)

Your answer should include:

▶ An introduction which talks about the main reasons for changing attitudes to poverty before 1906.
▶ A paragraph which discusses evidence for genuine concern for the poor as the reason for changing attitudes to poverty before 1906.
▶ A paragraph which discusses some evidence and other reasons why there were changing attitudes to poverty before 1906.
▶ A conclusion which is based on the evidence presented and addresses the question directly.

Planning your answer

▶ Your answer will draw on key information in Chapters 3–7.
▶ In small groups or pairs, brainstorm the information on evidence for:
   a) genuine concern for the poor as the reason for changing attitudes to poverty before 1906; and
   b) the evidence and other reasons why there were changing attitudes to poverty before 1906.
▶ Group the information into 'Genuine Concern Reasons' or 'Other Reasons' paragraphs.
▶ Find connections between the different pieces of information and group them together. This will give you a structure for the order in which you talk about the importance of genuine concern for the poor and other reasons why there were changing attitudes to poverty before 1906.
▶ Plan an overall response to the question.
▶ Show your plan to your teacher before starting your first draft.
▶ Edit your first draft and correct your mistakes.
▶ Rewrite the final draft of your answer.

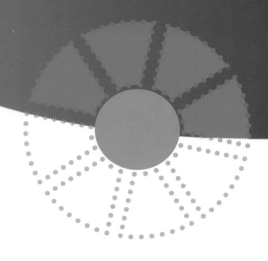

Chapter 8 How successful were the Liberal reforms at helping children?

What is this chapter about?

One of the biggest areas of the Liberal reforms concerned children. The Liberals thought that by helping children they would solve poverty in the long term as well as the short term.

By the end of this chapter you will be able to:

▸ Describe the social reforms for children that involved school meals and medical inspections.
▸ Describe the social reforms that made up the Children's Charter.
▸ Explain the effects of the social reforms on children.

Why was the Meals for Children Act passed?

The School Meals Act for children was the first reform passed by the Liberal Government to attack the problem of poverty. The government chose this reform because the Boer War and the poor condition of many recruits had scared the government about how fit future volunteers for the army would be. The government wanted to make sure British children would grow up to be healthy adults, because that would mean fit and strong soldiers and workers who would strengthen the British Empire.

The Schools Meals Act – its official name was the Education (Provision of Meals) Act – was passed in December 1906. The Liberal Government had supported a reform suggested by a Labour Member of Parliament (MP). This shows the importance of the new Labour MPs in pushing for social reform, even at this early stage.

What did the School Meals Act do?

▶ It allowed local education authorities to provide school meals for poor children.
▶ It allowed local authorities to pay for the school meals by charging a local tax (called a rate).
▶ Children from better-off families were expected to pay for their own school meals.

Why was this Act important?

By providing free school meals, the government was for the first time taking some responsibility for helping to feed the children of the poor. This reform challenged the idea of self-help. Supporters of self-help had long argued that families should look after their own children and if the children went hungry it was the fault of the parents.

As the historian Derek Fraser says:

SOURCE 8.1

The Government was little by little accepting responsibility for poverty caused by sickness, unemployment and hunger. From small reforms like meals for children, greater developments grew.

Derek Fraser

To begin with, the Act was not a success. The Act was voluntary, which meant that many local authorities chose not to provide food for the children. By 1913, over half the education authorities in England and Wales did not provide school meals. The problem was how to pay for the school meals. This was a problem that the government partly addressed in 1914 by providing money to meet half the cost of the meals.

It was also very difficult to judge who deserved a school meal or not. As a result, more children than expected were given meals.

Some people objected to the School Meals Act. They argued that providing school meals was too expensive. They also argued that giving the poor this kind of help undermined their independence and self-reliance. Critics believed this was a problem which would only get worse when the children grew up, became parents themselves and expected the government to help in times of hardship.

Why was the Medical Inspection Act passed?

The reasons for medical inspections were similar to those that had led to the School Meals Act. Medical inspections for children were introduced because of the need to improve Britain's health. This had been recommended by the Report of the Physical Deterioration Committee in 1904. The Committee had been set up to look at the reasons why Britain performed badly in the Boer War.

Since all children now had to go to school, it seemed sensible to check the children's health while at school. A new law was suggested to start medical inspection of children at school, which led to the 1907 Education Act. However, there was a problem with the reform as it only inspected children and reported on the illnesses they suffered from; it did not provide treatment for the illnesses. It was up to parents to pay for any medical treatment – and that could be expensive! To deal with this problem, some clinics were set up in schools to provide treatment. From 1912 the government provided money to pay for health clinics in schools.

Why was this Act important?

▶ The state had taken another big step towards looking after its **citizens**; in this case, children.

▶ The idea of 'self-help' was again being questioned and changed.

▶ The help given to children in poverty was seen as a step towards giving more and better healthcare for all people in Britain.

GLOSSARY

Citizen a person with rights and responsibilities

SOURCE 8.2

Another step had been taken towards a general medical service. Importantly, the government helped pay for the medical clinics.

From Derek Fraser, The Evolution of the British Welfare State (2003)

SOURCE 8.3

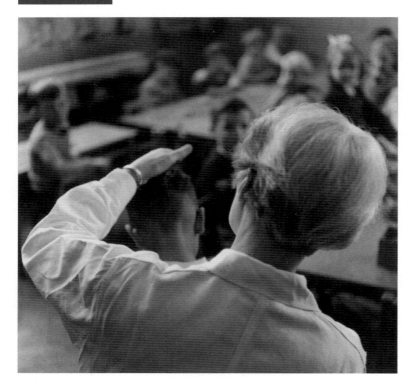

A medical inspection of school children taking place.
The hair is being checked for head lice.

Activity 1

What progress in medical care was made by the Education Act of 1907? You should describe three points of information. (N5 British AS 2.1)

What was the Children's Charter, 1908?

The 1908 Children's Act was the idea of a Liberal MP called Herbert Samuel. It is often called the Children's 'Charter' because a charter was a document that gave people certain rights or made rules clear. The Act brought together many earlier laws about children and specified how children should be protected and looked after.

The Children's Act clearly stated what the legal rights of children were:

▶ If children were not cared for properly by their parents, then the government should care for them.
▶ Children were banned from buying cigarettes under the age of 16 and were not allowed in pubs under the age of 14.
▶ It was forbidden to give alcohol to children under the age of five, except in the case of illness.
▶ It allowed for the inspection of children's homes.
▶ It ordered parents to put fire guards in front of open fires because 1,000 children every year died from burns after their clothes caught fire.
▶ Child criminals were no longer to be sent to prisons with adults. The Act set up special **juvenile courts** and the **borstal** system.
▶ The death sentence for children was abolished.

> **GLOSSARY**
>
> **Juvenile courts** special courts for young people
>
> **Borstals** youth detention centres

Why is this Act important?

▶ It protected children from abuse.
▶ Responsibility for children and how they were being brought up was being supervised by the government. Again, self-help was being challenged.

How successful were the Liberal reforms for children?

What they did	What they didn't do
Free school meals: one decent meal a day for children paid by local tax.	School meals NOT compulsory until 1914.
14 million school meals provided by 1914.	Not all local authorities provided school meals for the poor.
By 1914 the government were providing local authorities with grants to cover half the costs.	By 1914 only half the education authorities in England and Wales provided the service.
Education Act 1907: compulsory medical inspections at school.	They didn't give help to children during school holidays.
Children's Charter 1908: aimed to protect children from abuse and neglect.	Education Act 1907: free medical treatment was not compulsory; often ignored by education authorities; did little to solve problems until 1912; did not address the health problems of adults or school leavers.
The Charter gave legal protection for young people; the beginning of major government action in the lives of people.	Children's Charter: the ban on the sale of alcohol and cigarettes didn't really work; the borstal system failed in its attempt to solve youth crime; the system was brutal and often helped cause, rather than stop, re-offending among young offenders.

Chapter summary

▶ School meals were introduced for the poor but many local authorities did not provide them due to cost.
▶ Medical inspection of children was introduced. This identified the problem but did not provide a cure.
▶ The Children's Charter provided legal protection for children.
▶ All these Acts were important in showing how the state was increasing its role in the lives of children. Some people argued that this took responsibility away from the parents.

Activity 2

Priority pyramid

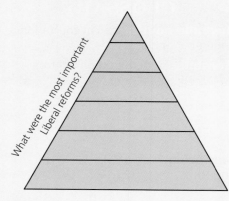

This task is to help you summarise the main points in this chapter and decide on the most effective reforms. Work in small groups.

1 Research the main reforms and how each helped children. Note these down in your workbook or work file. Decide which reforms were the most important.
2 Take a large piece of paper. Draw a triangle on the full size of the paper like the template given. Divide the pyramid into 'levels'. You can have as many levels as you need.
3 Write the Liberal reforms and how they helped children on the triangle. Most important reforms go at the top, least important at the bottom.

Activity 3

Revolving circle

1 Write a paragraph of 100–200 words on the question 'How successful were the Liberal reforms for children?'
2 Divide your class into two groups and form each group into a circle. One group makes an inner circle and the other group makes an outer circle. You should face each other, standing opposite a classmate.
3 Take it in turns to exchange your information with each other for approximately one minute. Give your classmate a red, amber or green rating and at least one suggestion for information they might have included.
4 The inner circle rotates clockwise and the outer circle rotates anticlockwise. The new pair repeats the process.
5 The rotation continues until you have had the opportunity to share information with at least two classmates.

Question practice

NATIONAL 4

SOURCE A

The Liberal reforms had some successes, but there were limits to what they did for children. On the one hand, the Liberal reforms introduced free school meals and also medical inspections for children; on the other, there was no help for children in the school holidays. Also, reforms that banned the sale of cigarettes and drink to young people did not work.

1 **Organise the information in Source A into 'benefits' and 'drawbacks' of the Liberal reforms for children. (N4 British AS 1.1/1.2)**

Success criteria

You should give at least two points of information in your own words.

NATIONAL 5

This task is intended to help you practise the 8-mark question in the external exam.

1 **To what extent were the Liberal reforms for children successful in dealing with the problem of poverty? (8 marks)**

Your answer should include:

▶ An introduction which mentions there were benefits and limitations to the Liberal reforms for children.
▶ A paragraph which discusses the benefits of the Liberal reforms for children.
▶ A paragraph which discusses the limitations of the Liberal reforms for children.
▶ A conclusion which is based on the evidence presented and addresses the question.

Planning your answer

▶ In small groups or pairs, brainstorm the benefits and the limits of success of the Liberal reforms for children.
▶ Group the information into 'Benefits' or 'Limitations' paragraphs.
▶ Find connections between the different pieces of information and group them together. This will give you a structure for the order in which you talk about the success of the Liberal reforms.
▶ Plan an overall response to the question.
▶ Show your plan to your teacher before starting your first draft.
▶ Read through your work carefully and mark any mistakes you spot with a green pen, then correct your work before handing it to the teacher.
▶ Rewrite the final draft of your answer.

Success criteria

Knowledge

- Make a judgement about the success of the Liberal reforms for children.
- Your answer must provide a balanced account of the benefits and the limits of success of the Liberal reforms for children.
- Up to five marks are given for the relevant knowledge used to address the question.
- One mark may be given for each accurate point that is properly explained.
- You can get a further mark for each point by developing its detail or explanation.
- A maximum of three marks are allocated for relevant knowledge used to address the question where only one factor or only one side of the argument is presented.

Structure

- Up to three marks can be given for presenting the answer in a structured way, leading to a reasoned conclusion which addresses the question.
- One mark may be given for the answer being presented in a structured way. The information should be organised and mention different factors.
- One mark may be given for a valid judgement or overall conclusion.
- One mark may be given for a reason being provided in support of the conclusion.

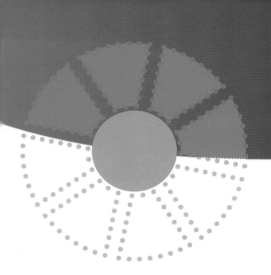

Chapter 9 How successful were the Liberal reforms at helping the elderly?

What is this chapter about?

The social investigator Charles Booth showed how much poverty was caused when people became too old to work. Old age pensions were introduced in 1908. They were important because they extended the help given by the government to those in need. The old age pension helped many, but was far from perfect.

By the end of this chapter you will be able to:

▶ Explain why old age pensions were introduced.
▶ Describe what old age pensions were paid.
▶ Explain what the reform achieved and its limitations.

Why were old age pensions introduced?

Once people had stopped working they did not earn money. Many elderly people had not been able to save when they worked because they did not earn enough money and their families could not always afford to look after them. Often, elderly people had no choice but to go into the workhouse under the Poor Law system. This was humiliating, especially for married couples who had to spend their final years apart from their partner.

Social investigators like Charles Booth supported the introduction of pensions as a way of making sure that old people had enough money to live independently. In 1895, Booth gave evidence to the Royal Commission on the Aged Poor, where he proposed the pension scheme:

SOURCE 9.1

The scheme that I propose to the Commission intends that everyone shall be entitled to an old-age pension of 5 shillings a week from age 65.

Charles Booth (1895)

There was a lot of support for old age pensions. Pressure for reform came from a number of places:

▶ Most people thought that old age pensions were a good idea.
▶ The Royal Commission on the Aged Poor, in 1895, had provided evidence which supported the idea of old age pensions.
▶ Countries such as New Zealand and Germany had already introduced pensions for the elderly by 1906.
▶ The Labour Party and trade unions supported the introduction of pensions.
▶ By 1908, the Liberals had lost MPs to the Labour Party in a series of **by-elections**. Some people in the Liberal Party thought that they would gain votes by providing a new old age pension law.

> ### GLOSSARY
> **By-election** an election for an MP in between general elections

Lloyd George said:

SOURCE 9.2

It is time we did something that appealed straight to the people – and help stop this loss of MPs to Labour, and that is most necessary.

Lloyd George

Activity 1

Look at Source 9.2. Explain why Lloyd George wanted to introduce the old age pension. You should explain at least one reason. (N4 British AS 2.2)

What did the Act do?

▶ The pension was to be paid for from general taxes. No contributions had to be made by those who got the pension.
▶ The pension was paid to people over 70 years of age.
▶ The full rate pension was worth 5 shillings a week to a single person and 10 shillings a week for a married couple.
▶ The amount of money paid as a pension depended on how much money the person getting the pension had already saved.
▶ Payments were made through the Post Office.

Why was this Act important?

▶ Old people did not have to make contributions to get the old-age pensions. Again the self-help idea of individuals saving for old age had been swapped for government action.

Lloyd George explained why he thought it was important that people should not have to pay towards a pension scheme:

SOURCE 9.3

There are two reasons why the elderly should not have to pay towards the old-age pension. In the first place, it would exclude most women from its benefits because they don't earn enough. We know this because there is only a small number of women who are members of the friendly societies. Most women don't earn anything at all. The second *reason is that most working men are unable to spare enough money from their weekly earnings to pay for old age in addition to that which they are making for sickness, **infirmity**, and unemployment.*

Lloyd George

GLOSSARY

Infirmity physical or mental weakness

Activity 2

Explain why Lloyd George thought people should not have to pay towards the pension scheme. You should give three pieces of evidence in your own words. (N5 British AS 1.1/2.1)

SOURCE 9.4

Why do you think elderly people preferred getting their pensions from the Post Office?

Payments are made to the elderly at a Post Office

The *Manchester Guardian* newspaper reported the first payment of pensions:

SOURCE 9.5

The first payments under the Old-age Pensions Act were made yesterday at post-offices. Probably about half a million needy old people were made glad yesterday by the first payment of a pension which will last for the rest of their lives. It is not surprising to read that many of the recipients expressed heartfelt thanks to the post-office clerks who handed them their money.

Manchester Guardian

SOURCE 9.6

THE NEW YEAR'S GIFT.

A child bringing the gift of old age pensions to an elderly couple

Payment of pensions was made through the Post Office where other business, such as selling stamps, took place. This treated people with dignity, unlike if they went to the workhouse. Many more people claimed the pension as a result.

How successful were the Liberal reforms for old people?

What they did	What they didn't do
Guaranteed an income for those too old to work.	Old age pensions came nowhere near meeting the basic needs of the elderly.
Made life slightly better for those who were poor and elderly.	Level of pension set too low to live on: 2 shillings below the 'poverty line'.
There was a high uptake and many people were grateful for their pension.	Many people did not reach the age of 70 to benefit from the system.
No contributions were required – pensions were given as a right.	Too many qualification rules stopped people in need from claiming. These rules still made moral judgements about who deserved help, e.g. no pension if you'd been in prison.
During 1906–14, there was a 75 per cent decrease in old people entering the poor house.	Cost of pensions was bigger than the government had planned for. They had expected to spend £6.4 million but pensions cost £8.5 million in the first year. This caused problems for the government as they had to find the money from somewhere.
By 1914 nearly 1 million people were applying for the pension.	

Chapter summary

SOURCE 9.7

▶ Many different groups agreed that old age pensions were a good idea.
▶ Old age pensions were paid to people over the age of 70.
▶ Payments were made from taxation; no contribution had to be made.
▶ The Act was popular and cost more money than the government thought it would.

What is the attitude of the cartoonist to Lloyd George?

THE PHILANTHROPIC HIGHWAYMAN.

Mr. Lloyd-George. "I'LL MAKE 'EM PITY THE AGED POOR!"

Punch cartoon

Activity 3

Finish the story

Imagine you are the old person getting their old age pension in Source 9.4.

1 Work in small groups. Discuss what this lady's life might have been like before she got her pension and the difference getting the pension might have made to her life.
2 Share your ideas with the rest of the class.
3 Your teacher will read out part of the old lady's diary – the day on which she got her pension.
4 You need to continue the diary where the teacher left off. Each member of the group should take it in turns to complete the diary entry.
5 Share your ideas with the rest of the class.

Success criteria

Each story should cover:

▶ what this lady's life might have been like before she got her pension
▶ the difference getting the pension might have made to her life.

Each group member should contribute to the story.

Activity 4

Plus, minus, interesting

Review the information in this chapter on the successes and limitations of the Liberal reforms for the elderly. Work in small groups.

A plus = a benefit

A minus = a drawback

Interesting = a main information point

▶ Research at least three each of 'Plus, Minus, Interesting' points of the Liberal old age reforms. Write these on Post-its and rank them in order of importance.

▶ Share your ideas with the rest of the class.

▶ Write your findings in your workbook or work file.

Question practice

NATIONAL 4

SOURCE A

The Liberal reforms did much for old people. From 1908, the poor had access to weekly pensions. Those who got pensions had not had to contribute towards them. However, the pension was not enough to live on. People did not qualify for a pension until they were 70 and most poor people died before this age.

1 **Organise the information in Source A into 'Benefits' and 'Drawbacks' of the Liberal reforms for old people.** (N4 British AS 1.1/1.2)

Success criteria

You should give at least two points of information in your own words.

NATIONAL 5

1 **Explain the reasons why old age pensions were introduced by the Liberal Government in 1908.** (5 marks)

This is an 'explain' question. This means you must give five reasons why something did or did not happen. It is not enough to just write down facts no matter how correct they are. You must link each fact back to the question, explaining how that fact did or did not allow something to happen. For this question, this means you need to explain why the economy and poverty worried people.

To get you started on your answer, here are some hints:

▶ Explain why social investigators like Charles Booth helped cause the reforms.

▶ Explain how evidence from the Government Royal Commission helped change ideas on help to the elderly.

▶ Explain why examples from abroad helped cause the old age reforms.

▶ Explain why support from the Labour Party and the trade unions helped cause the Liberal old age reforms.

▶ Explain why rivalry with the Labour Party helped cause the old age reforms.

Success criteria

▶ Include five factual pieces of information on why old age reforms were introduced.

OR

▶ Include at least three developed pieces of information on why old age reforms were introduced.

▶ Give accurate and detailed pieces of information that are properly explained.

In her village, Flora Thompson saw the reaction to pensions. One old person was so happy that she got confused and called David Lloyd George, the man behind the idea of pensions, 'Lord George':

SOURCE A

When old age pensions began life was transformed for old villagers. They were relieved of worry. They were suddenly rich. Independent for life! At first when they went to the Post Office, tears of gratitude would run down the cheeks of some. They would say as they picked up their money, 'God bless that Lord George and God bless you, miss'. They gave flowers from their gardens and apples from the trees for the Post Office girls who handed them the money.

2 Evaluate the usefulness of Source A as evidence of the reaction to the payment of old age pensions. (6 marks)

Success criteria

▶ For a mark to be given, you must identify an aspect of the source and make a comment that shows how this aspect makes the source more or less useful.

▶ Up to four marks may be given for points about **author**, **type of source**, **purpose** and **timing**.

▶ Up to two marks may be given for your evaluation of the content of the sources which you consider are useful in terms of the proposed question. For full marks to be given each point needs to be discretely mentioned and its usefulness explained.

▶ If you list information, that will be considered to be one point and will get only one mark.

▶ Up to two marks may be given for the application of relevant and developed pieces of recalled information. This has to be relevant to the question for full marks to be given.

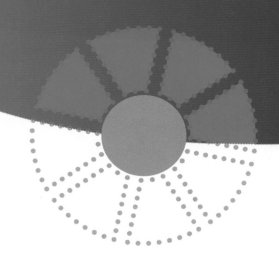

Chapter 10 How successful were the Liberal reforms at helping the sick and the unemployed?

What is this chapter about?

This chapter is about the reforms to help the sick and the unemployed. These reforms were very important but they did not help all who found themselves in poverty due to sickness and unemployment.

By the end of this chapter you will be able to:

▶ Explain the idea of insurance.
▶ Describe how the first part of the 1911 National Insurance Act helped the sick.
▶ Explain why the first part of the 1911 National Insurance Act is so important.
▶ Describe the work laws passed by the Liberals.
▶ Describe the introduction of labour exchanges, 1910.
▶ Describe how the second part of the National Insurance Act helped the unemployed.
▶ Explain how successful the Liberal reforms for sickness and unemployment were.

Why did the Liberals introduce reforms for the sick and unemployed?

Lloyd George wanted to help more than just children and the elderly. He also wanted to help those who became poor through ill-health and unemployment. He was especially interested in those affected by ill-health. Bad health cost many workers their jobs, and eventually their lives. Lloyd George's own father had been a victim of tuberculosis, which at this time killed 75,000 people a year.

What was the Insurance Scheme?

The Liberals planned an insurance scheme in which the employer, employee (worker) and government would contribute to a fund of money when the worker was employed, or in good health. When the worker was unable to work, amounts of money were paid out to the worker for a limited period of time. This money was to help the worker through a difficult period when they could have fallen into poverty.

Insurance was popular with the Liberals as a way of paying for reforms because:

▶ Insurance meant the government did not have to pay the full cost.
▶ It allowed workers to contribute to their own care. This gave workers a sense of pride as they were not getting 'something for nothing'. It made the scheme 'respectable'.
▶ A similar system, which covered health, had been working well in Germany since the 1880s.
▶ It was also hoped that grateful workers would vote Liberal in return for the help provided.

Why was there opposition to the Insurance Scheme?

▶ The government's scheme competed with Friendly Societies who ran their own schemes to save for times when workers were ill.
▶ Trade unions objected to the fact that working men were being expected to contribute to the reform.
▶ Private insurance companies, such as the Prudential, were threatened by the competition from the government scheme.
▶ The House of Lords did not like the Liberals and tried to delay the reform.
▶ Doctors worried about the increasing role of government. The head of the **British Medical Association** attacked the reforms. He said that it stopped individuals making an effort and would cost too much money to run.

> **GLOSSARY**
> **British Medical Association** the doctor's professional organisation

Lloyd George was forced to make compromises because of the opposition to his plans for insurance.

▶ He had to drop benefits for widows and orphans. This won over the big insurance companies.
▶ The Friendly Societies were allowed to run the Government Insurance Scheme.

How did the Liberals try to help the sick?

| The National Insurance Act: Part I: Sickness | |
Payments	Benefits
Employees contributed four pence a week if they earned under £160 a year.	10 shillings a week for 13 weeks and 5 shillings for another 13 weeks if ill.
Employers contributed three pence a week.	Free medical treatment from a doctor chosen by a local Insurance Commission.
The government contributed two pence a week.	30 shillings maternity benefit for the birth of each child. (There were 12 pence in a shilling, and 20 shillings in a pound in British currency at this time.)
Contributions were recorded by placing stamps on cards.	

It gave workers '9 pence for 4 pence' in contributions according to Lloyd George, as Source 10.1 shows.

SOURCE 10.1

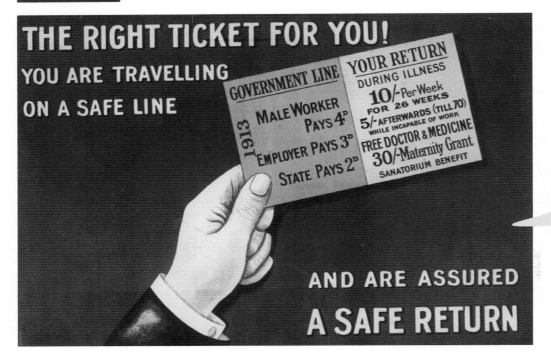

THE RIGHT TICKET FOR YOU!
YOU ARE TRAVELLING ON A SAFE LINE

GOVERNMENT LINE
1913
MALE WORKER PAYS 4ᴰ
EMPLOYER PAYS 3ᴰ
STATE PAYS 2ᴰ

YOUR RETURN
DURING ILLNESS
10/- Per Week FOR 26 WEEKS
5/- AFTERWARDS (TILL 70) WHILE INCAPABLE OF WORK
FREE DOCTOR & MEDICINE
30/- Maternity Grant
SANATORIUM BENEFIT

AND ARE ASSURED A SAFE RETURN

How was the government trying to appeal to workers?

Government poster showing what was paid and the benefit received

Some thought the reforms did not go far enough. The Labour MP, Keir Hardie, thought that a married woman should get the same benefits as her husband:

SOURCE 10.2

The benefits being given to the wage earner will relieve poverty due to sickness to a certain extent. But it is not just the wage earner whose illness affects the whole family. When the wife is sick, it is nearly always necessary to pay for outside help. The sick wife might need nursing, the housework needs to be done and young children require to be looked after. All of this needs to paid for, for the pay of the husband is not enough on its own.

Keir Hardie

Activity 1

In your own words, explain why Keir Hardie thought the sickness reforms didn't go far enough. You should give three points of information. (N5 British AS 1.1)

THE COMING OLYMPIC STRUGGLE.
Active Training for the Passive Resistance Event.
[July 3, 1912.]

A cartoon in Punch magazine shows that both employers and servants objected to the Insurance Act. The punch bag has Lloyd George's face on it.

How successful were the Liberal reforms for the sick?

What they did	What they didn't do
Gave workers security and peace of mind.	No provision for hospitals.
Workers were now more likely to seek medical assistance rather than wait for a problem to get worse.	Dependants (other members of the family) were not included in the scheme.
10 million men and 4 million women were covered by the scheme.	Flat rate contributions (everyone paying the same) hit the poor harder than the rich:
The government had extended its role to help the poor in society.	After using up their 26 week entitlement, ill workers had to rely on the Poor Law medical facilities.
The Act was a compulsory one.	Only the person who paid the contribution was entitled to these benefits – other family members got no benefits if they fell ill.
	Many workers were angry at being forced to contribute money because it reduced their wages.
	The Liberals did not get the electoral benefits they hoped for. The Insurance Act was blamed for the loss of at least two MPs in parliament as angry workers voted for other political parties before 1914.

How did the Liberals help the unemployed?

What were labour exchanges?

In 1908 the Labour Exchange Act was passed and on the 1 February 1910, 83 labour exchanges opened across the country. Winston Churchill visited 17 on the first day they opened. They were run by government officials with the aim that unemployed workers could go there to find work. Employers would also go to these exchanges in order to find workers if they needed them. The idea was a good one and the number of exchanges grew quickly. By 1911 there were 414 exchanges in operation helping workers find jobs. Exchanges also offered a place for workers to mend their clothes and washing facilities for them to get clean.

What were the problems with labour exchanges?

▶ Employers did not have to tell the exchanges they had vacancies.
▶ Workers did not have to register with the exchanges if they were out of work.
▶ Manual and casual labourers didn't use the labour exchanges as much as skilled workers so the poorest workers didn't get the most help. This was because you had to be able to read and write quite well to use the exchange.

SOURCE 10.4

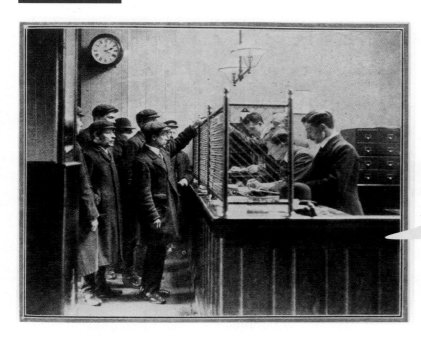

How did the labour exchanges help people?

Workers looking for jobs at one of the first labour exchanges at Camberwell in England

What help was given to the unemployed?

Unemployment help was similar to health insurance, with employer, employee and the state making weekly contributions into a fund of money. Once a worker had paid in enough they had the right to withdraw money from this fund. The National Insurance Act came into operation on the 15 July 1912.

The National Insurance Act: Part II: Unemployment	
Payments	Benefits
Employees contributed 2½ pence per week.	7 shillings a week for up to 15 weeks.
Employers contributed 2½ pence per week.	A week's benefit was paid for every five weeks of contributions made.
The state contributed 1⅔ pence per week.	Benefit was paid through the labour exchanges.

Why was there opposition to the Liberal unemployment reforms?

There was opposition to the Liberal unemployment reforms mainly because of the cost and because some resented government 'interference'. There were a number of high profile protests in Scotland alone:

SOURCE 10.5

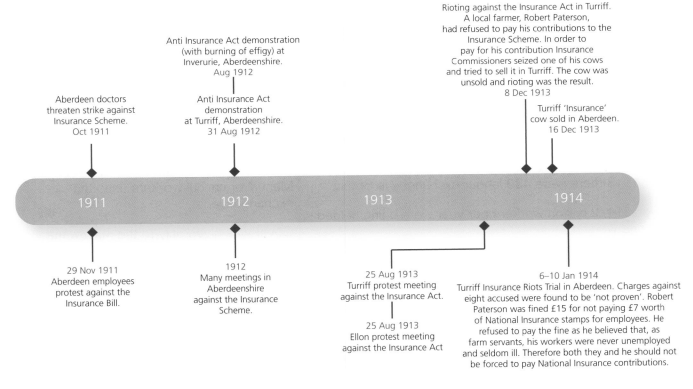

A timeline of opposition to the Insurance Act

SOURCE 10.6

Would you have sympathised with the farmer or the government?

'The Turra Coo'. This was a cow seized from a local farmer for non-payment of his insurance contributions. Local supporters bought back the cow and returned it to the farmer.

How successful were the Liberal unemployment reforms?

What they did	What they didn't do
By 1913 there were 430 labour exchanges in Britain.	Manual or casual workers used the exchanges least.
By 1914, 2 million workers per year were being helped to find work.	Cover was given only to the main wage earner.
Gave the workers who were covered temporary relief from poverty.	Benefit cut off after 15 weeks for 'not genuinely seeking work' even if there was no work in the area.
2.25 million workers covered.	Only 2 million workers covered.
Trades covered were building, construction, shipbuilding, mechanical engineering, iron founding, vehicle construction and saw milling.	The level of benefit was linked to contributions.
The scheme was unique. No similar scheme had been introduced anywhere else in the world.	Only some trades were covered – almost all skilled men.
No judgement was made about being 'deserving' or 'undeserving' of help.	
The role of government in people's lives was extended.	
The reforms recognised that unemployment had complex causes.	

The unemployment reforms only intended to help certain trades. The minister who presented the reforms to parliament said:

SOURCE 10.7

The House may ask why particular trades were chosen. These were the trades in which we found the biggest variations in employment. They were the trades most sensitive to ups and downs of the economy.

SOURCE 10.8

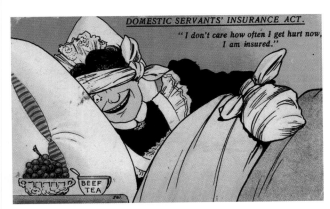

The Act was very important. These postcards were produced in support of the National Insurance Act.

Chapter summary

▶ Health insurance required contributions from employee, employer and the state. Benefits were paid out when enough contributions had been made.
▶ Health insurance provided cover for the person contributing. The rest of the family was not covered in the event of ill-health.
▶ Health Insurance saw the government taking more responsibility for looking after people in Britain.
▶ The Liberals passed reforms that helped reduce the hours of work and guaranteed minimum levels of pay in certain jobs.
▶ Labour exchanges were opened to help unemployed men to find jobs. The exchanges were popular but mostly used by skilled labourers.
▶ The National Insurance Act (Part II) covered men in certain jobs that suffered from short periods of unemployment.
▶ The Act only covered the worker and once the entitlement was used up the Poor Law had to be used.
▶ Opposition to the Insurance Act continued for some time in parts of the country.

Activity 2

Summarise this chapter

▶ Put the heading: 'Liberal reforms for the sick and unemployed' in your workbook or work file.
▶ Draw a table like the one below. Remember, your table will need to be bigger than the one below to include all your information.
▶ Find out at least two pieces of key information about each subheading.

	Key information
Reasons for the reforms	
The Insurance Scheme	
Opposition to the Insurance Scheme	
The Liberal sickness reform	
The labour exchanges	
The Liberal unemployment reform	

Activity 3

Each one, teach one

Your topic is the 'Liberal reforms for the sick and unemployed'. Find a space big enough for you to move about easily so that you can interact and do this activity freely. On your own, choose a particular fact or event from Activity 2 and write it on a Post-it. Your teacher may check with you to ensure that there is a spread of different statements across the whole class. Practise reading your fact or event out loud to check that you understand its meaning.

Draw a clock at the back of your workbook or work file and put 3, 6, 9 and 12 on it. Make 'appointments' with four people in your class for each of these time slots. Your teacher will allocate a period of time for each 'appointment'.

Move around and share your fact or event with your 'appointments', making sure that you explain it fully. Listen to and learn the fact or event that your 'appointment' explains.

Return to your own desk and write down all the facts and events that you have learned in your workbook or work file. You should record at least another three key facts or events about the Liberal sickness and unemployment reforms.

Hold a class discussion on which facts or events were the most interesting and which were easiest or hardest to remember – and why.

Question practice

SOURCE A

The Liberals introduced an insurance scheme for sick workers. The worker, employer and government all paid into a sick fund. When the worker had paid in enough money, he was able to claim benefits if he couldn't work.

1 **Describe the Liberal reforms for the sick.** (N4 British AS 2.1)

Success criteria

You should give two points of information in your own words.

SOURCE B

In 1909, the Liberals set up Labour Exchanges. These were good because for the first time there was a place where people could look for work. But casual or manual workers did not use the exchanges much because you needed to read and write quite well. The Liberals also passed a reform giving help to some people if they became unemployed. This helped stop the worker and his family sliding into poverty. However, only some trades were covered by this scheme.

2 **Organise the information in Source B into 'Benefits' and 'Drawbacks' of the Liberal reforms for the unemployed.** (N4 British AS 1.1/1.2)

Success criteria

You should give at least two points of information in your own words.

Source C is about the unemployment reforms passed by the Liberal Government.

SOURCE A

Previous ways of helping the unemployed had only reached a minority of workers. The Liberal solution was a national unemployment insurance scheme. Workers, employers and the government all contributed to an unemployment fund. The worker had to contribute a certain amount before he could make a claim. The scheme did not intend to cover the whole workforce but just those trades that were prone to seasonal unemployment or downturn in trade.

1 **How fully does Source A describe the Liberal unemployment reforms, 1906–14?** (6 marks)

Success criteria

▶ Place the source in context by explaining information in the source and applying that information to your own knowledge.

▶ Up to two marks may be given if only the source or recall is given.

▶ Up to three marks may be given for explaining pieces of information from the source.

▶ Up to four marks may be given for explaining pieces of information from your own knowledge which are relevant to the question asked.

▶ Pieces of information from your own knowledge can be used as further explanation of information in the source or as new points.

The following task is intended to help you practise the 8-mark question in the external exam.

2 **To what extent were the Liberal reforms successful in dealing with the problem of sickness and unemployment?** (8 marks)

Your answer should include:

▶ An introduction which mentions that there were benefits and also limitations to the Liberal reforms for sickness and unemployment.

▶ A paragraph which discusses the benefits of the Liberal reforms for sickness and unemployment.

▶ A paragraph which discusses the limitations of the Liberal reforms for sickness and unemployment.

▶ A conclusion which is based on the evidence presented and addresses the question.

Planning your answer

▶ In small groups or pairs, brainstorm the benefits and the limits of success of the Liberal reforms for sickness and unemployment.

▶ Group the information into 'Benefits' or 'Limitations' paragraphs.

▶ Find connections between the different pieces of information and group them together. This will give you a structure for the order in which you talk about the success of the Liberal reforms.

▶ Plan an overall response to the question.

▶ Show your plan to your teacher before starting your first draft.

▶ Read through your work carefully and mark any mistakes you spot with a green pen, then correct your work before handing it to the teacher.

▶ Rewrite the final draft of your answer.

Success criteria

Knowledge

▶ Make a judgement about the success of the Liberal reforms for sickness and unemployment.

▶ Your answer must provide a balanced account of the benefits and the limits of success of the Liberal reforms for sickness and unemployment.

▶ Up to five marks are given for the relevant use of knowledge to address the question.

▶ One mark may be given for each accurate point which is properly explained.

▶ You can get a further mark for each point by developing its detail or explanation.

▶ A maximum of three marks are allocated for relevant knowledge used to address the question where only one factor or only one side of the argument is presented.

Structure

▶ Up to three marks can be given for presenting the answer in a structured way, leading to a reasoned conclusion which addresses the question.

▶ One mark may be given for the answer being presented in a structured way. The information should be organised and mention different factors.

▶ One mark may be given for a valid judgement or overall conclusion.

▶ One mark may be given for a reason being provided in support of the conclusion.

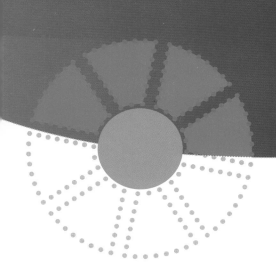

Chapter 11 What opposition did the Liberals face in carrying out their reforms?

What is this chapter about?

The social reforms passed by the Liberals cost more money than first thought. The government had to find a way to pay for the new social reforms **plus** other expenses such as the arms race with Germany just before the First World War. The only solution was to raise taxes. However, the House of Lords was against the social reforms and did not want increased taxes. The story of how the Liberals overcame the House of Lords is important in explaining the success of the Liberal reforms.

By the end of this chapter you will be able to:

▶ Explain why the Liberals needed more money.
▶ Explain the budget of 1909.
▶ Explain why the House of Lords was against the Liberal reforms.
▶ Describe how the Liberals overcame the House of Lords.

Why did the Liberals need more money?

Old age pensions had cost the government much more money than they expected. At the same time, Britain had to find the money to pay for the naval arms race caused by the launch of the Dreadnought in 1906. Britain also had increasing rivalry with Germany over trade and colonies. The government needed to find more money to pay for this spending. This meant that the people of Britain would have to pay more in the way of taxes.

What was the 1909 Budget?

Lloyd George needed to raise £16 million to pay for pensions and ships. He decided to do this by:

▶ Increasing the tax paid on the income people earned. The amount varied depending on how much you earned. The better off were expected to pay more.
▶ Introducing a super tax on incomes over £3,000 each year.
▶ Introducing higher taxes (called duties) on tobacco, beer, spirits and petrol.
▶ Introducing a land tax of 20 per cent on the increase in land value when land was sold.
▶ Introducing a tax on undeveloped land and minerals.

Lloyd George thought this budget was very important. When he made a speech to parliament on the budget he said:

SOURCE 11.1

This is a War Budget. It is for raising money to wage war against poverty and squalor.

Lloyd George

Activity 1

Explain why Lloyd George wanted to introduce the 1909 Budget. You should explain one point. (N4 British AS 2.2)

In the 1909 budget Lloyd George wanted the rich, especially wealthy land owners, to pay more taxes. These taxes were then to be spent on helping the poorer in society. Many Conservative politicians opposed Lloyd George's attempt to 'redistribute wealth'.

In the House of Commons the Conservatives were outnumbered by the Liberals, but in the House of Lords the Conservatives held a majority. Many of the Conservative Lords were landowners who were very annoyed at the proposals to tax their land. In November 1909 they rejected the budget by 350 votes to 75.

The Liberal Government was faced with a crisis. The Liberals attacked the unelected House of Lords for overturning a decision made by the elected House of Commons. They argued the House of Lords wanted wealth for themselves and were willing to let the people of Britain down.

Lloyd George attacked the Lords, saying:

SOURCE 11.2

Should 500 men, ordinary men chosen accidentally from among the unemployed (someone in the House of Lords inherited their title and did not need to work due to their wealth), override the wishes of millions of hard-working people? Who made 10,000 people (the land owners in Britain) the owners of the soil, and the rest of us trespassers in the land of our birth?

Lloyd George

Activity 2

Explain why Lloyd George attacked the House of Lords. You should explain two points. (N5 British AS 2.2)

SOURCE 11.3

RICH FARE.

THE GIANT LLOYD-GORGIBUSTER: "FEE, FI, FO, FAT,
I SMELL THE BLOOD OF A PLUTOCRAT;
BE HE ALIVE OR BE HE DEAD,
I'LL GRIND HIS BONES TO MAKE MY BREAD."

Punch cartoon

Do you think the cartoonist has a positive or negative attitude to Lloyd George?

The Liberal Prime Minister, Herbert Asquith, called an election over the 'People's Budget' in January 1910. The Liberals won a majority with their allies in the Labour Party and Irish Nationalists. The budget proposals were passed by the House of Lords and became law after this victory.

The Liberals were determined to make sure that the House of Lords could never again threaten laws passed by the House of Commons. A second general election was held in December. The Liberals and their allies won again. They introduced the Parliament Bill to curb the power of the House of Lords. The king threatened to create a Liberal majority in the Lords if it did not pass the Parliament Bill. After this threat the Parliament Act was passed in 1911. The House of Lords could no longer stop laws passed by the House of Commons.

The two elections of 1910:

SOURCE 11.4

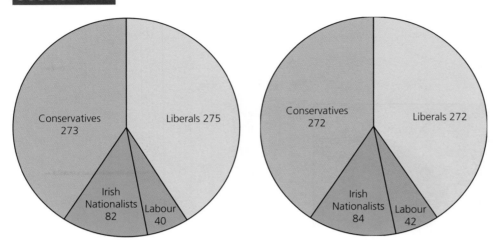

Left: January 1910 election results; right: December 1910 election results

What did the 1911 Parliament Act do?

The Parliament Act said that:

▶ The House of Lords could only delay new laws passed by the House of Commons for two years, not reject them.
▶ The House of Lords could not delay finance bills (the budget).
▶ The social reforms of the Liberals could continue without opposition from the Lords.

Chapter summary

▶ Old age pensions cost more than the government had planned for.
▶ The government also had to pay for new expensive battleships.
▶ The budget to pay for these was rejected by the House of Lords.
▶ After a long struggle, the power of the House of Lords was reduced by the Parliament Act, 1911.

Activity 3

Mind mapping

Put the heading: 'Why did the Liberal Government need more money for its social reforms?' in your workbook or work file. Create a mind map of the main reasons why the Liberals needed more money.

Activity 4

Walk around, talk around

Work in pairs or in small groups. Take a large piece of paper and draw a triangle that fills most of the page. Allow space for you to write outside the triangle.

Your teacher will allocate a period of time. Fill the triangle with as many main points about the 1909 Budget as possible. Once your time is up, leave your paper and move on to the next group's paper.

Your teacher will allocate another period of time. Add more information to the new group's paper on the outside of the triangle. Keep moving round until all the information is on the paper or the paper is filled.

Review all the main points about the 1909 Budget with the rest of the class.

Question practice

NATIONAL 4

SOURCE A

The 1909 Budget increased taxes on the rich to pay for the social reforms. Hardest hit were wealthy landowners. There were also taxes on goods like tobacco and alcohol.

1 Look at Source A. Describe what the 1909 Budget did. (N4 British AS 2.1)

Success criteria
You should give two points of information in your own words.

NATIONAL 5

1 Describe how the Liberals overcame the power of the House of Lords. (5 marks)

You would not get a source to help with this question in the exam, but use the following prompt card to help get you started:

Prompt card
▶ Lloyd George's attacks on the House of Lords
▶ Two general elections in 1910
▶ Intervention of the king
▶ The 1911 Parliament Act.

Success Criteria
▶ Include five factual pieces of information on how the Liberals overcame the power of the House of Lords.
OR
▶ Include at least three developed pieces of information on how the Liberals overcame the power of the House of Lords.
▶ Give accurate and detailed pieces of information that are properly explained.

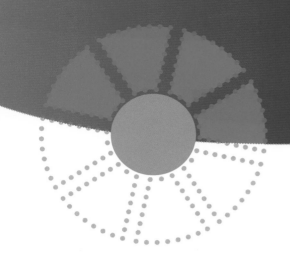

Chapter 12 To what extent did the Liberal reforms solve the problem of poverty?

What is this chapter about?

This chapter aims to make an overall assessment of the success of the Liberal reforms. We will look at the ground-breaking ideas it introduced and its limitations in dealing with the problem of poverty.

By the end of this chapter you will be able to:

▶ Describe the limitations of the Liberal reforms.
▶ Explain the important ideas it introduced (insurance, 'contribution', pensions funded from direct taxation).
▶ Describe the different views of historians.

What were the limitations of the Liberal reforms?

The historian Edward Royle has commented:

SOURCE 12.1

The Liberal Reforms showed a more humane understanding of poverty. They tried to remove the respectable and deserving poor from the control of the Poor Law.

Edward Royle

The Liberal reforms tried to provide help for people in a way that did not bring shame to the poor. This was very different from the old Poor Law.

However, the Liberal reform programme had many limitations:

▶ Local authorities did not *have* to provide school meals.
▶ Medical inspections for children identified problems, it didn't cure them.
▶ Old age pensions were limited to the over 70s.
▶ Health insurance only covered the worker *not* their family.

▶ Labour exchanges were voluntary *not* compulsory.
▶ Unemployment benefit was for a very limited number of industries.

Some reforms were resented by many of the people they were intended to help. The National Insurance Act in particular led to opposition. As one recent historian puts it:

SOURCE 12.2

Liberalism got relatively little political credit from the workers, who resented having to pay the contributions.

> Why do you think some people were fed up with the Liberal social reforms?

Some people thought there had been enough social reform in Britain.

What were the successes of the Liberal reforms?

The Liberal reforms were important because they marked a big change in how governments thought people in poverty should be helped.

The reforms introduced important ideas.

▶ The state became directly involved in young people's lives.
▶ Old age pensions were financed from general taxation.
▶ The insurance idea was introduced to help fund some of the social reforms.
▶ Pensions were collected from the Post Office, removing the shame of the Poor Law.
▶ Unemployment benefits were paid by the labour exchanges, not through the Poor Law system.

Some people in the Liberal Government of 1906–14 clearly wanted to continue reforming. From 1908 Winston Churchill was proposing a wide-ranging series of reforms that included:

1 Labour exchanges and Unemployment Insurance
2 National Infirmity Insurance
3 Modernising the Poor Law
4 Compulsory education up to the age of 17.

If it had not been for the outbreak of war in 1914, more reform seems to have been planned.

What do historians think about the Liberal reforms?

Historians disagree about the reforms and what they were trying to do. Some think that the Liberal reforms were the starting point for reforms in the future, in particular, the Labour reforms after the Second World War.

What are the positive views of the Liberal reforms?

SOURCE 12.3

*Two young politicians, David Lloyd George and Winston Churchill, were responsible both for reviving the Liberal Government after 1908 and for launching a great social programme which laid the foundations of the future **Welfare State**.*

From C. Cross, The Liberals in Power (1963)

GLOSSARY

Welfare State the series of social reforms between 1945 and 1951 that aimed to provide care for people in need 'from the cradle to the grave'

SOURCE 12.4

From 1906 to the beginning of the First World War there was great activity in the field of social reform. In fact, it would be true to say that most of the developments that we now think of as part of the Welfare State are built on the foundations laid during this exciting time.

From G. Williams, The Coming of the Welfare State *(1967)*

What are critical views of the Liberal reforms?

An alternative view is that the Liberal reforms were very limited in their aims: we should not claim that they laid the foundations for the future Welfare State.

SOURCE 12.5

Whilst historians agree that overall the Liberal reforms helped those targeted, they also agree that many people continued to 'slip through the net'.

From D. Peaple, S. Lancaster, T. Lancaster, British History, 1876–1918 *(2000)*

SOURCE 12.6

Many of those who created the Liberal reforms had no thought of creating a 'welfare state' of the type which developed in Britain after 1945. Indeed many of the Liberals of 1906–14 would have disliked the idea of a welfare state.

From J.R. Hay, The Origins of the Liberal Welfare Reforms *(1975)*

Activity 1

In your own words, explain the positive and negative opinions of historians on the Liberal reforms. You should mention three points. (N5 British AS 1.1/1.2)

What are the balanced views of the Liberal reforms?

Other historians have tried to steer a middle way between these two views:

SOURCE 12.7

One cannot escape the conclusion that Liberal social policy before the First World War was both a break with the past and an anticipation of radical changes in the future.

From Derek Fraser, The Evolution of the British Welfare State *(2003)*

The social reforms of the pre-war Liberal government had no chance to make a major dent in poverty before the First World War broke out, but there is some evidence to suggest that they and some reforms in the 1920s which developed from them began to make a difference in the long term.

Peter Murray, Poverty and Welfare, 1815–1950 (2006)

How successful were the Liberal reforms overall?

What they did	What they didn't do
First government effort to deal with the causes as well as the effects of poverty: young, sickness, unemployment and old age.	Break the link between making contributions and being deserving of help in times of need. You still had to pay in, to get money out.
Established the expectation of government action to help people in need.	Help most women workers who didn't work in the jobs covered by the Liberal reforms.
Extended government action in people's lives beyond solving poverty; reforms passed to help the employed:	In the short-term, the Liberal reforms made life harder for low-paid workers because insurance contributions meant workers got less money in their pay packets.
The 1906 Workman's Compensation Act helped six million workers who could now claim compensation for injuries and diseases which were the result of working conditions.	Help the really poor and unskilled workers because they could not afford to contribute.
In 1908, coalminers secured an eight-hour working day.	Deal with major issues causing poverty like housing and access to further education.
The 1909 Trade Boards Act set up trade boards to fix minimum wages. This gave some protection to workers in trades like tailoring and lace making.	Provide long-term help to those in need.
The 1911 Shops Act limited working hours and guaranteed a weekly half-day holiday.	
The 1911 Parliament Act broke the power of the House of Lords in favour of the democratically elected House of Commons, which furthered democracy.	
The ground-breaking reforms meant that all future governments would have to consider more social reform.	

Chapter summary

▶ The Liberal reforms were a change in how the government treated the poor.
▶ The Liberal reforms had both strengths and weaknesses in the amount of help that was given to the poor.
▶ Historians disagree about the significance of the reforms.
▶ Some Liberals were planning further reforms before war broke out in 1914.

Activity 2

The following questions go up in level of difficulty in pairs. The first two are easy. The last two are hard. How many will you try to do?

1 What social problems did the Liberal reforms try to deal with?
2 Describe the Liberal reforms for old people.

3 What help was given to the sick and unemployed?
4 What was done to help employed people?

5 What were the limitations of the Liberal reforms?
6 'The Liberal reforms were ground-breaking.' Do you agree or disagree with this statement? You will need to be able to support your answer with evidence.

Activity 3

A spider diagram can help you to summarise the information on the success of the Liberal reforms. You can choose to do the planning for this task in pairs or small groups, but it would be a good idea to complete the spider diagram on your own in your workbook or work file. This will give you a learning check on how well you know the information.

Using a large piece of paper, make notes on 'Successes of Liberal reforms' and 'Limits of Liberal reforms'.

If you work in threes, one person can read, one person can listen and summarise, and one person can write down the information. Make sure you include at least four pieces of information for each heading.

Take a double page in your workbook or work file and record the information you have researched in a colourful and well-presented spider diagram.

Question practice

NATIONAL 4

SOURCE A

The Liberal reforms tried to deal with the problem of poverty. The big reforms were focused on helping the young, old, sick and unemployed. These groups got special help or pensions in time of need. However, some have criticised the reforms and not everyone was helped by the reforms. Also, people often had to make contributions to get help when they needed it. Even when the government gave pensions to old people, the amount was not enough to live on.

1 How well did the Liberal reforms deal with the problem of poverty? Draw a table of the 'successes' and 'limits'. (N4 British AS1.1/1.2)

Success criteria
You should give at least two pieces of information in your own words.

NATIONAL 5

Sources A and B are about the success of the Liberal reforms, 1906–14:

SOURCE A

The Liberal reforms were the beginning of more reforms in the twentieth century. They helped solve some of the worst problems of poverty. For the first time, old people over the age of 70 were given pensions to live on. Medical inspections and school meals were given to the young. The sick and unemployed got help when they were not working. This stopped them sliding into poverty.

SOURCE B

The Liberal reforms set the pattern of later reforms. The Liberals focused on the big causes of poverty identified by Booth and Rowntree. Many reforms helped the young. These included free school meals and the 1908 Children's Charter. Pensions were paid to the elderly. Importantly, these were given as of right after the age of 70. Workers in certain industries got sickness and unemployment benefits from 1911. These were intended to help the worker until he could work again.

1 **Compare the views in Sources A and B on the success of the Liberal reforms.** (4 marks)

Success criteria

▸ You should interpret evidence from the source.
▸ Make direct comparisons between the information in the sources.
▸ You can get up to two marks for comparing how far the two sources agree or disagree overall.
▸ You can get up to four marks for making direct comparisons between the information in the two sources.
▸ 'Source A says … and Source B agrees …' will get one mark. A developed comparison: 'Sources A and B agree that the Liberal reforms helped old people. Source A says … and Source B agrees, saying …' will get two marks.

The following task is intended to help you practise the 8-mark question in the external exam.

2 **To what extent did the Liberal reforms deal successfully with the problem of poverty?** (8 marks)

Your answer should include:

▸ An introduction which mentions there were benefits and limitations to the success of the Liberal reforms.
▸ A paragraph which discusses the benefits of the Liberal reforms.
▸ A paragraph which discusses the limitations of the Liberal reforms.
▸ A conclusion which is based on the evidence presented and addresses the question.

Planning Your Answer

In small groups or pairs, brainstorm the benefits and the limits of success of the Liberal reforms.

Group the information into 'Benefits' or 'Limitations' paragraphs.

The following timeline should remind you of the main reforms:

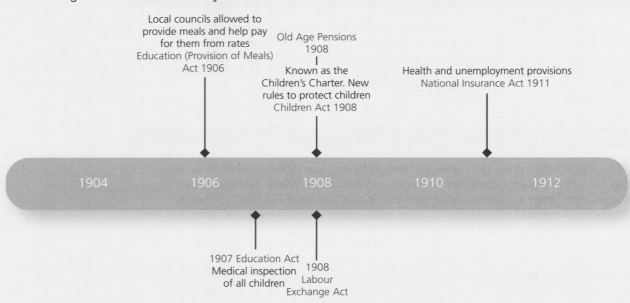

- ▶ Find connections between the different pieces of information and group them together. This will give you a structure for the order in which you talk about the success of the Liberal reforms.
- ▶ Plan an overall response to the question.
- ▶ Show your plan to your teacher before starting your first draft.
- ▶ Read through your work carefully and mark any mistakes you spot with a green pen, then correct your work before handing it to your teacher.
- ▶ Rewrite the final draft of your answer.

Success criteria

Knowledge

- ▶ Make a judgement about the success of the Liberal reforms for sickness and unemployment.
- ▶ Your answer must provide a balanced account of the benefits and the limitations of the Liberal reforms for sickness and unemployment.
- ▶ Up to five marks are given for relevant knowledge used to address the question.
- ▶ One mark will be given for each accurate point that is properly explained.
- ▶ You can get a further mark for each point by developing its detail or explanation.
- ▶ A maximum of three marks are allocated for relevant knowledge used to address the question where only one factor or only one side of the argument is presented.

Structure

- ▶ Up to three marks can be given for presenting the answer in a structured way, leading to a reasoned conclusion which addresses the question.
- ▶ One mark may be given for the answer being presented in a structured way. The information should be organised and mention different factors.
- ▶ One mark may be given for a valid judgement or overall conclusion.
- ▶ One mark may be given for a reason being provided in support of the conclusion.

Chapter 13 What happened to welfare reform between 1914 and 1939?

What is this chapter about?

When the First World War ended Lloyd George had promised 'a land fit for heroes', but many returning soldiers and their families were disappointed. The 1920s and 1930s were years of economic problems and high unemployment. The government could not afford more social reforms. There were also cuts in the help that had been provided for the poor.

By the end of this chapter you will be able to:

▶ Explain the impact of the First World War on **welfare reform**.
▶ Describe the failure of inter-war welfare plans.
▶ Explain the effects of the economic slump after 1929.
▶ Explain the impact of failure to reform on attitudes to welfare.

 GLOSSARY
Welfare reform the help given to resolve social problems, e.g. poverty

What progress was made during the First World War?

The First World War again underlined the need to improve the physical fitness of the nation. When conscription for the army was introduced in 1916, it was found that out of every nine recruits, only three were fully fit to fight.

By the end of the war, government involvement in every aspect of people's lives had hugely increased. DORA (The Defence of the Realm Act) 1914 gave the government wide powers. New ministries were set up to cope with wartime problems. By 1918, the Ministry of Food rationed basic foods, such as tea and butter, so that everyone got a fair deal. Taxes were put up and important industries such as coal and the railways were taken under government control.

Lloyd George's Government also had plans to carry out important welfare reforms:

SOURCE 13.1

Out of justice to the living and out of respect to the dead, we are called to rebuild the national life on a better and more enduring foundation.

Why did post-war welfare plans fail?

SOURCE 13.2

Explain why this ex-soldier is protesting.

Ex-soldier protesting at the failure of the government to deliver its promises of jobs

Lloyd George had won the general election of 1918 promising a 'land fit for heroes', but big changes did not happen for several reasons:

▶ The 1918 election produced a **coalition government** between the Liberals and the Conservatives. The Conservatives did not want more social reform.
▶ The First World War caused damage to Britain's economy and so caused unemployment. That meant the money raised from the taxes of workers went down so the government had less money to spend on welfare policies.
▶ There were five different governments between 1918 and 1929. This meant that there was no time to put plans into action.

> **GLOSSARY**
>
> **Coalition government**
> a government made up of more than one political party

What were the effects of the economic slump after 1929?

From 1929, a trade slump that started in the USA spread across the world. This caused high unemployment in Britain, which led to an increase in poverty. By 1931, there was a real crisis in Britain.

In 1929, a Labour Government had been elected. It was led by Prime Minister Ramsay MacDonald. He asked a committee, led by Sir George May, to come up with a plan to deal with the crisis. May said that the government had to cut spending and suggested cutting the wages of people who worked for the government. He also said that there should be a cut in unemployment benefit. Many people in the Labour Party could not accept this and resigned from the government.

Ramsay MacDonald then formed a new coalition 'National Government' with the Conservatives and some Liberals and the spending cuts were made. Unemployment benefits were reduced by 10 per cent. After 26 weeks, more money was paid out after a 'means test'. MacDonald and others were thrown out of the Labour Party for agreeing to the cuts.

The benefit cuts were eventually restored in 1934.

The means test

The local authority carried out an investigation into everything a family owned or earned. Even the old age pension of a grandparent or a small amount earned by a child was considered. Any money coming into the household led to a cut in the amount of benefit paid. It was a humiliating experience and forced families to live apart so that they could keep their unemployment benefit. The working poor hated the means test.

SOURCE 13.3

What does this protest tell you about how unemployed men felt?

This is the 1934 hunger march. Unemployed men walked to London to protest at the lack of jobs and the way they were being treated

What action did the government take after 1931?

In 1932, a Royal Commission was set up to investigate unemployment benefit. It recommended that a proper national system be set up. There were to be two national boards: one to pay out money to those who had paid National

Insurance contributions, and one to take care of those who had not. These recommendations were put into practice with the 1934 Unemployment Act.

The government realised that it would have to do more than just pay unemployment benefit. They would have to take action to try to prevent unemployment. Government Training Centres for the unemployed were set up. Areas of high unemployment were given 'special area' status. It was hoped this would encourage investment. However, Government Training Centres did not guarantee jobs and the 'special areas' were not very successful at attracting new firms.

SOURCE 13.4

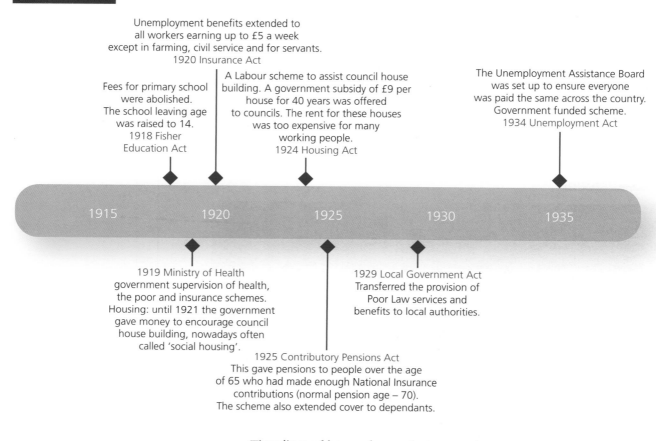

Timeline of key reforms between the wars

What progress had been made by 1939?

By 1939, the government had begun to realise that it was not enough to react to crises. Instead, it had to try to prevent problems such as unemployment.

Charities worked in partnership with the government under the National Council for Social Services.

The social problems for which people could get help had increased. Social services now included housing and education as well as poverty and health.

There was more awareness of the big differences between rich and poor in Britain. Writers such as J.B. Priestley, who had done a tour of Britain in 1934, helped influence the desire for more community action.

Chapter summary

▶ The First World War increased government powers.
▶ Expectations of big post-war changes failed to happen owing to economic and political crises.
▶ The government took more responsibility for social services.
▶ There was more pressure for state action to solve social problems.

Activity 1

If this is the answer, what is the question?

Below you will find a list of words or names. You have to make up a question that can only be answered by the words in the list. For example, if the words were 'First World War', the question might be 'When did the government increase their control over the British people?' Write the question and answer into your workbook or work file.

▶ Land fit for heroes
▶ Britain's economy
▶ Unemployment
▶ 1924 Housing Act
▶ 1929
▶ The National Government
▶ The Means Test
▶ 1934 Hunger March
▶ 1934 Unemployment Act
▶ 'Special areas'

Activity 2

Summarise this chapter

Write a short summary of this chapter describing the main things that have happened. You must use *all* the words listed in Activity 1 in as few sentences as possible. Your title is: 'What social reforms happened between 1918 and 1939?'

Chapter 14 What was the impact of the Second World War on welfare reform?

What is this chapter about?

The Second World War brought together people of different classes who in peacetime had little to do with each other. Many middle-class and upper-class people saw poverty and other social problems they had not been aware of before. During the war, there were many government schemes and reforms to ensure that the health and fitness of the nation was kept up. The war led to a determination to create a better future for Britain once the war was over. Historians continue to debate the exact impact of the Second World War on causing the development of the Welfare State after 1945.

By the end of this chapter you will be able to:

▶ Explain the effects of war on the home front and government.
▶ Explain the effects of evacuation and German bombing.
▶ Describe rationing and its effects.
▶ Describe how the war increased government control over people's lives.
▶ Describe some important social reforms during the Second World War.
▶ Describe the different points of view of historians about the importance of the Second World War to welfare reform in Britain.

What was the effect of war on life in Britain?

The Second World War broke out in 1939 but serious fighting did not start until 1940. It was clear that the war was going to last some time. During the war a new national mood developed; people were determined to beat Hitler and create a better Britain.

How did the government change?

Soon after the start of the war, Winston Churchill replaced Neville Chamberlain as Prime Minister. He created a government that included members of all the main political parties. By working with other political parties, Churchill hoped to show Britain's determination to defeat Hitler.

Several members of the Labour Party were given important jobs as government ministers. Clement Attlee became the Deputy Prime Minister. Ernest Bevin, leader of the Transport and General Workers' Union, was given the job of Minister of Labour. This was an essential job in organising the war effort at home. Labour was the party that had made further welfare reform an important part of their policies. Now they had a chance to get experience of government and making decisions.

SOURCE 14.1

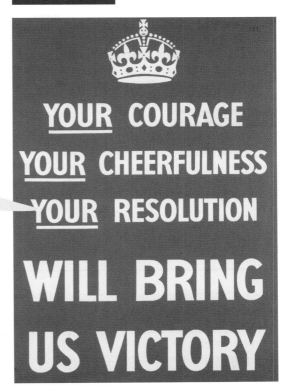

A government poster from the Second World War

What do you think was the purpose of the poster?

How did evacuation change people's attitudes to welfare reform?

SOURCE 14.2

What do you think the parents of the children would have been feeling?

Evacuees queuing for buses in Glasgow Road, Clydebank, 1941

For years people had lived with the fear that if there were a war, 'the bomber would always get through'. This meant that bomber aircraft would blast cities and kill thousands of people. The government organised the evacuation of children away from high risk areas where they lived, such as industrial and dockland areas. When children from the slum areas were evacuated to safer, and better off areas, the people who took the children into their houses were shocked by the bad health and bad clothing of the children. As the *Perth Advertiser* reported:

SOURCE 14.3

The group of kids had been very neglected. They had to just strip the clothes off them and wash them. They had a big, hot bath ready. But this wee lad wasn't going to go into that bath and he screamed and yelled some words over and over again, and spread his arms and legs so they couldn't get him into the bath. Lady Elgin asked the housekeeper 'What is he saying?' The housekeeper replied, 'He's saying it's ower effin' deep and its ower effin' hot.'

Perth Advertiser, 20 September 1939

Most of the evacuation took place at the beginning of the war. There were two main effects of evacuation:

1 Different social classes met up and socialised with each other in a way unheard of in peacetime;
2 It raised awareness of continuing social problems, which many assumed had disappeared.

Both of these helped to unite Britain and give its people a common experience and purpose.

How did the bombing change people's attitudes to welfare reform?

Soon after the start of war, the Germans started to bomb London and the big industrial towns in Britain. Manchester, Liverpool and Coventry all suffered heavy damage. In Scotland, Aberdeen was the most bombed city, with 34 attacks. Glasgow, Dundee and Edinburgh were also targeted, and Clydebank suffered devastating damage over two nights of bombing.

Very often the bombers missed their targets, resulting in damage to civilian areas. The bombing destroyed the homes of rich and poor alike. It brought together people who normally had little to do with each other. Those made homeless had to find places to stay in the homes that were left. The bombings helped to develop community spirit – a feeling that people should look out for each other.

SOURCE 14.4

How did the bombing help develop community spirit?

A bombed building in Central London

SOURCE 14.5

What message is the cartoonist trying to give about the bombings?

A wartime cartoon showing Goering's Luftwaffe bouncing off the East End of London

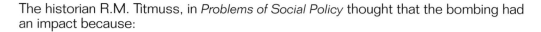

The historian R.M. Titmuss, in *Problems of Social Policy* thought that the bombing had an impact because:

SOURCE 14.6

Damage to homes and injuries to persons were not less likely among the rich than the poor. The help provided by the government was offered to all groups in the community. The pooling of national resources and the sharing of risks were the guiding principles.

R.M. Titmuss, Problems of Social Policy (1950)

Activity 1

Look at Source 14.6. Explain the impact of the Second World War on people's attitudes. You should make two relevant points. (N5 British AS 2.2)

How did rationing change people's attitudes to welfare reform?

In peacetime, Britain depended on imports – 60 per cent of its food came from abroad. Those food supply lines into Britain were cut by the Nazis and the shortages caused queuing and rising prices. In people's minds, it was unacceptable for some wealthier people to get better treatment and food supplies when everyone was fighting the war. The daily threat of bombing combined with shortages of both supplies and workers meant that everyone had to have their lives directed by the government.

In April 1940, Lord Woolton became the Minister of Food. He realised that if everyone was to get a balanced diet then the government would have to control food production and supplies. The Ministry of Food's job was not just about making sure everyone got a fair share of the food. It also aimed to improve the nation's health in order to improve the ability to fight. The Ministry of Food even added vitamins and minerals like calcium and iron to certain foods.

The priority was to ensure 'fair shares for all' and to avoid waste. To ensure 'fair shares for all', the government introduced food rationing in 1940 and clothes rationing in 1941.

Miss C.M. Edwards, from Lincolnshire, wrote in her diary in 1943:

SOURCE 14.7

I think the food authorities have done a wonderful job. There's really no shortage anywhere of essentials.

Miss C.M. Edwards (1943)

Activity 2

Look at Source 14.7. Explain the success of rationing in Britain. You should make one point. (N4 British AS 2.2)

Throughout the war, the Ministry of Food organised an advice and propaganda campaign. They published a series of 'Food Facts' leaflets giving recipes and advice on how to eat healthily. In April 1940, the National Food Education Campaign was launched. This involved nationwide cookery demonstrations to help women make the most of home-produced foods.

Why is the Ministry of Food important?

▶ The Ministry of Food is important as evidence of the increase in government control during the Second World War.
▶ Its activities established that the government should be responsible for promoting the nation's health.
▶ The Ministry of Food was the first national attempt to promote healthy eating in the world. After the war it attracted visiting nutritionists from other countries because it had done such a good job.
▶ The work of the Ministry of Food continued after the Second World War. Food rationing for products such as meat lasted until 1953. Bread rationing did not stop until 1946 owing to the shortage of cereals. Advice on nutrition has continued to the present day.

How did conscription change people's attitudes to welfare reform?

Conscription was introduced for young men in the armed services. People could also find themselves conscripted to work in essential industries such as coal mining and farming. The biggest change in the workplace was experienced by women. Britain was the only country during the Second World War to conscript women for the war effort. Unmarried women could be called up to the armed forces and other women directed to work elsewhere. They replaced men in jobs, and played a vital part in ensuring that food production was maintained.

The experience of conscription in Britain is important because it helped people to accept that the government should direct all resources, including people, for the common good. This was an important idea behind the Welfare State.

SOURCE 14.8

British women working on the railways, circa 1943

Why would women not have been doing this job before the Second World War?

How did the Second World War increase government control of the economy?

During the Second World War there was also a change in the government's approach to managing the economy. The cost of the fighting forced the government to abandon its pre-war ideas of minimum tax and spending. Taxes were increased and Britain became heavily reliant on the 'Lend-Lease' loans from America. One of Churchill's expert advisers was the economist J.M. Keynes. He believed that it was the government's responsibility to ensure that Britain's economy would be successful. In particular, he believed that a successful economy should provide full employment for its people. He thought the only way to do that was by government action and public spending. His ideas were influential during the Second World War and after.

Planning for the future – The Beveridge Report

The Second World War showed up serious underlying social problems in British society. It was recognised that there was a need for a general system of help for poorer people, organised and paid for by the state. In 1942, a plan was published that at last seemed to answer that need. It was called the Beveridge Report, and offered an overall plan for the British system of welfare.

What were the main changes in welfare during the war?

SOURCE 14.9

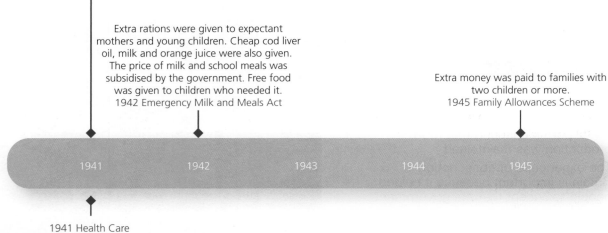

The hated inquiry into all the earnings of an unemployed man's family was done away with.
1941 Abolition of Means Test

Extra rations were given to expectant mothers and young children. Cheap cod liver oil, milk and orange juice were also given. The price of milk and school meals was subsidised by the government. Free food was given to children who needed it.
1942 Emergency Milk and Meals Act

Extra money was paid to families with two children or more.
1945 Family Allowances Scheme

1941 | 1942 | 1943 | 1944 | 1945

1941 Health Care
War wounded (including bomb victims) were given free treatment. 'Emergency beds' were also provided that were paid for by the state. Free immunisation programme against diptheria greatly decreased the number of deaths.

1941 Supplementary Payments Scheme
Extra help was given to old age pensioners who found it hard to manage.

A timeline of key changes in welfare

How did the Second World War help cause the Welfare State?

▶ The wartime Coalition Government included Labour ministers in important positions who carried on their work when Labour became the government in 1945.

▶ The sense of community created by the war made people determined to create a better society after the war.

▶ The government took a much greater role in helping people.

▶ The British public expected their government to do more for them.

▶ Evacuation had revealed how bad poverty was in the cities to those who lived outside.

▶ Pressure to plan to rebuild Britain after the war had led to Churchill's Coalition Government drawing up plans to tackle some of the giant social problems identified in the Beveridge Report, 1942.

Evidence for the impact of the Second World War comes from a survey carried out by the Government's Mass Observation department. Trained investigators asked people about the changes that they expected to see after the war as a result of the 'total war':

Mass observation survey 'Top Six'	
Change	Percentage of people expecting this as a major post-war trend
Fewer class distinctions	29
More government control	21
Education reform	19
More equal incomes	15
More social services	14
Less dictatorship; 'fascism'	13

Activity 3

Describe in your own words, the social and political changes people expected to see after the Second World War. (N5 British AS 1.1)

But historians have disagreed about how important the Second World War was in causing welfare reform. Some historians such as D. Gladstone in *The Twentieth-Century Welfare State* believed:

SOURCE 14.10

Almost all the ideas and proposals for reform in social security and education, for example, had been discussed in the 1920s and 1930s.

D. Gladstone, The Twentieth-Century Welfare State

On the other hand J. MacNicol argued:

SOURCE 14.11

The sheer scale of the events that took place during those six crucial years seems to lend credibility to the view that modern wars are a major force behind progressive social change.

J. MacNicol

Activity 4

How important was the Second World War in causing the development of the Welfare State? You should identify two perspectives before making a judgement about it. (N5 British 2.2/2.3)

Chapter summary

▶ Bombing, evacuation and rationing raised awareness of continuing social problems.
▶ The Second World War united the different communities and classes of Britain with a common aim.
▶ The war caused the government to get more involved in all areas of people's lives.
▶ The Ministry of Food established the responsibility of the government to ensure the nation's health and a safe food supply.
▶ The suffering of the war caused a determination to deal with welfare problems once the war was over.
▶ Historians disagree about how important the Second World War was in causing the Welfare State.

Activity 5

Building a learning wall

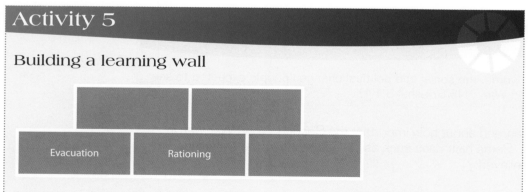

Create your own learning wall on why the Second World War helped cause the setting up of the Welfare State.

Work in pairs or small groups. Each group should write down their ideas about the effects of the Second World War. Each effect should be on a separate piece of paper or Post-it note. Each group should use their effects to construct their learning wall. You should work through the effects, deciding as a group on how relevant each effect is. Place the most important effects at the bottom of the wall and the least important effects at the top.

Groups should then give feedback on their decisions, justifying their choices if they are different from those of another group. You teacher might ask you to peer assess each other's work.

Activity 6

Creating a fishbone diagram

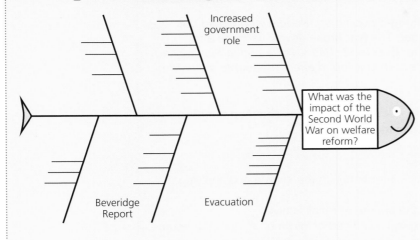

Create a fishbone diagram to explain in detail how the Second World War helped create the Welfare State.

Copy the artwork onto an A4 sheet of paper (or bigger, if you like!) and write the following question at the tip, or nose, of the skeleton: 'What was the impact of the Second World War on welfare reform?'

Write the answers to the question on your diagram, with the main findings running along the main fish bones. Write along the smaller horizontal bones to add in further detail about the main findings. Some have been filled in for you already.

Question practice

NATIONAL 4

SOURCE A

When they came we were full of good will. And we thought, 'Oh the poor dears coming from the towns will be so pleased to come to this beautiful country place' ... But one lady was very cross at being given children who were infected with head lice.

1 **Describe the reaction of country people to evacuees in your own words.**
   (N4 British AS 1.1/2.1)

Success criteria
You should give two points of information in your own words.

SOURCE B

In peacetime, people always tend to look out for themselves – a 'me first' situation. In the war this was different. Everybody felt they should do what they could for someone else. If someone was bombed out, the nearest family took them in.

2 **Explain how the Second World War changed the way people behaved.** (N4 British AS 2.2)

Success criteria
You should give one point of information in your own words.

NATIONAL 5

SOURCE A

The big thing about the war was that it mixed people up. People who would not normally meet, lived and worked together. The war broke down the class and occupational barriers that existed before. Everybody had a value and in that sense all men and all women were equal. This had a profound effect on people's attitude to social and economic problems.

1   How fully does Source A show how the Second World War changed people's attitudes towards social problems? (6 marks)

Success criteria

▶ Place the source in context by explaining information in the source and applying that information to your own knowledge.
▶ Up to two marks may be given if only the source or recall is given.
▶ Up to three marks may be given for explaining pieces of information from the source.
▶ Up to four marks may be given for explaining pieces of information from your own knowledge which are relevant to the question asked.
▶ Pieces of information from your own knowledge can be used as further explanation of information in the source or as new points.

Source B is from a diary by Sergeant Ernie Teal about his experiences fighting in Europe in 1944–45.

SOURCE B

When we got to Holland, we went to some of the houses. They had flushing toilets and nice gardens. They were just ordinary people but so much better off than we were. I was really taken aback. And when we got to Germany I thought 'these people have been living well under Adolf and I don't like Adolf'. I got ambitious for change. We owned two thirds of the world and we lived worse off than them.

2   Evaluate the usefulness of Source B as evidence of how the Second World War changed attitudes. (6 marks)

Success criteria

▶ For a mark to be given, you must identify an aspect of the source and make a comment which shows how this aspect makes the source more or less useful.
▶ Up to four marks may be given for points about **author**, **type of source**, **purpose** and **timing**.
▶ Up to two marks may be given for your evaluation of the content of the source which you consider are useful in terms of the proposed question. For full marks to be given each point needs to be discretely mentioned and its usefulness explained.
▶ If you list information, that will be considered to be one point and will get only one mark.
▶ Up to two marks may be given for the application of relevant and developed pieces of recalled information. This has to be relevant to the question for full marks to be given.

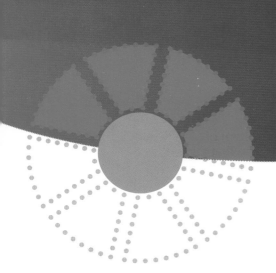

Chapter 15 What was the importance of the Beveridge Report?

What is this chapter about?

The Beveridge Report helped create the Welfare State that was set up between 1945–51. Beveridge not only identified the major social problems that needed to be solved, he also gave recommendations on what should be done. The report captured the popular feeling that living standards had to be better after the war. It raised expectations about what the government would do to help those in need.

By the end of this chapter you will be able to:

▶ Describe the 'five giants' of Want, Disease, Ignorance, Squalor and Idleness.
▶ Describe the main points of the Beveridge Report.
▶ Explain the reasons why the Beveridge Report was so important.

Who was Beveridge?

Sir William Beveridge was an expert on social welfare and unemployment problems. He had helped Churchill and Lloyd George create the labour exchanges and National Insurance laws during the Liberal Government, 1906–14.

During the Second World War, Beveridge chaired the committee that produced the 'Report on Social Insurance and Allied Services' in 1942. Beveridge used this report to set out his vision of welfare support 'from the cradle to the grave'. He identified five giant social problems facing Britain. The report went much further than Churchill wanted but was immediately popular with the British public. The Beveridge Report helped shape the social policy of both the wartime Coalition Government and the Labour Government after 1945.

What were the 'five giants'?

Beveridge had been asked to look at the question of providing a proper system of sickness and unemployment benefit to workers. However, Beveridge argued that such benefits were only part of the answer to achieving social progress. Beveridge said:

SOURCE 15.1

Social insurance may provide income security, it is an attack on Want. But Want is one of only five giants. The others are Disease, Ignorance, Squalor, and Idleness.

Sir William Beveridge

Beveridge believed that tackling just one of the five giants wouldn't do much good. If the welfare of the British people was to improve, then the government would have to try and solve all the problems that stood in its way.

In order to fight these giants Beveridge argued that it would be necessary to also provide a proper national health service and family allowances to mothers with children. Most importantly, the government should undertake a policy of full-employment.

The Beveridge Report was important because, for the first time, action on economic and social problems were linked.

The ideas contained in the Beveridge Report provided the basis for the policies of the Welfare State.

What were the main points of the Beveridge Report?

The report's main recommendations were:

- A government minister to be appointed to control all the benefit schemes.
- A National Health Service should be set up.
- People in work were to pay weekly national insurance contributions.
- Unemployed people to have the right to payments for an indefinite period.
- Payments to be made at a standard rate, without a means test.
- Benefits to include old age pensions, maternity grants, pensions for widows and people injured at work.
- Family allowances to be introduced.

Reaction to the Beveridge Report

The report was enthusiastically received – and not just by the public. In Parliament, 97 Labour and 22 Liberal and Conservative MPs voted for the report to be put into operation as soon as possible.

The fact that some MPs wanted immediate progress on the Beveridge Report at a time when the war effort was going so badly shows how important they thought the report was.

SOURCE 15.2

William Beveridge writing his report

The report gave people hope that things 'post-war would be better than pre-war' and that the war had been fought to make a better life for the people of Britain.

As one soldier remembered:

SOURCE 15.3

I was in a prisoner-of-war camp when the Beveridge report came out. Somebody had a copy sent to them, it caused a lot of excitement and there were big discussions and debates about why we had been fighting.

Not everyone was delighted with the Beveridge Report. Some people did not want the government's interference in their lives. Another view was that Beveridge's proposals would cost too much and the taxes required to fund the scheme would be too great. One historian, Peter Hennessy, has said:

SOURCE 15.4

The Treasury thought that Beveridge's proposals would break the bank. They thought that the taxes needed to pay for the scheme would be too heavy and have an negative effect on industrial activity.

From Peter Hennessy, Never Again

Why was the Beveridge Report important?

The Beveridge Report was important for three main reasons:

1 It had revolutionary ideas. Firstly, that society could, and should, fight the five giants of poverty. Secondly, that people not only had freedom to do things but the freedom *from* certain things, like want, disease, etc. Thirdly, that the scheme should be universal, that is, applied to everyone.

2 It established the principle that people were entitled to benefits as they had made insurance contributions when working. This took away the stigma of getting state help.

3 The scheme proposed was the same for everyone. All working people would pay the same into the scheme and get the same benefits. This meant that everyone got a fair deal.

The report was also important because of the effect it had on the 1945 election. In 1943, there was a debate in the House of Commons on the Beveridge Report. James Griffiths, a future Labour minister, put forward a motion asking that the full Beveridge Report be put into practice. From the debate, it was clear that the Conservatives in the government were less than enthusiastic about all of Beveridge's proposals. No Conservative MP voted for the motion.

The historian Peter Hennessy thinks that the Beveridge Report had a decisive effect on the 1945 election result because it set the 'battleground' for the election:

SOURCE 15.5

In the weeks before the general election both Labour and Conservatives were promising a full system of national insurance and health service as laid out by Beveridge. The question was which party could be most trusted to turn the fine words into reality.

From Peter Hennessy, Never Again

What progress was made towards the Beveridge Report before 1945?

The Labour Party is credited with putting the Beveridge Report into action, but the wartime Coalition Government did at least make a start with laws on education and family allowance.

In 1943, a ministry to supervise insurance benefits was set up. The Ministry of Town and County Planning was also set up in 1943 and immediately produced proposals for new towns to ease congestion around London. Temporary housing was built for the homeless. The price of building materials was controlled to stop house prices rising out of control.

The government also published a number of proposals on the National Health Service, employment policy and social insurance. All of these showed that the Coalition Government accepted much of the Beveridge Report. For the most part however, action taken by the Coalition Government was not especially far-reaching. Churchill wanted to concentrate on winning the war.

Chapter summary

▶ The Beveridge Report identified five key social problems to be solved: Want, Disease, Ignorance, Squalor and Idleness.
▶ The Beveridge Report recommended action on social and economic problems.
▶ The Beveridge Report was hugely popular and helped the election of Labour in 1945.
▶ The Beveridge Report had ground-breaking ideas that help should be universal, equal and fair.

Activity 1

Summarise this chapter

Take a whole page in your workbook or work file. Add the title: 'The Impact of the Beveridge Report'.

Now draw up a table with four columns headed, 'Main points of the Report', 'Reaction to the Report', 'Criticism of the Report' and 'Importance of the Report'. In each column list the key people and events.

Finally, write a short paragraph answering the following question: 'What was the impact of the Beveridge Report?' You will have to support your answer with evidence from the table you have drawn up.

Activity 2

Walk around, talk around

Work in pairs or small groups. Take a large piece of paper and draw a triangle that fills most of the page.

Your teacher will allocate a period of time. Fill the triangle with as many key points about the Beveridge Report as possible. Once your time is up, leave your paper and move on to the next group's paper.

Your teacher will allocate another period of time. Add more information to the new group's paper outside the triangle. Keep moving around until all the information is on the paper or the paper is filled.

As a class, discuss and confirm all the key information on the Beveridge Report.

All of the class should take part in discussing and recording information.

Question practice

Source A is from the Beveridge Report.

SOURCE A

Social insurance should be treated as one part only of a full policy of social progress. Social insurance fully developed may provide income security; it is an attack upon Want. But Want is only one of the five giants on the road of reconstruction and in some way the easiest to attack. The others are Disease, Ignorance, Squalor and Idleness.

1 Describe the social problems that Beveridge aimed to solve. (N4 British AS 2.1)

Success criteria

You should give two points of information or one developed point about the social problems that Beveridge aimed to solve.

SOURCE B

Interest in the Beveridge Plan on its publication was really tremendous. One report says there has been more widespread discussion on this than on any single event since the outbreak of war.

2 Describe the public reaction to the Beveridge Report. (N4 British AS 2.1)

Success criteria

You should give two points of information or one developed point about the public reaction to the Beveridge Report.

Source A is by a historian written in 1992.

SOURCE A

Government departments like the Treasury did not like the Beveridge report. They thought the reforms were too expensive and taxes might have to increase. In contrast, the public popularity of Beveridge soared. A survey carried out in 1943 showed 86 per cent in favour and only 6 per cent opposed to the Beveridge report. The proposal for a free health service had 88 per cent support overall, but only 81 per cent from the better off.

1 **Evaluate the usefulness of Source A as evidence of the reaction to the Beveridge Report.** (6 marks)

Success criteria

▶ For a mark to be given, you must identify an aspect of the source and make a comment which shows how this aspect makes the source more or less useful.
▶ Up to four marks may be given for points about **author**, **type of source**, **purpose** and **timing**.
▶ Up to two marks may be given for your evaluation of the content of the source which you consider are useful in terms of the proposed question. For full marks to be given each point needs to be discretely mentioned and its usefulness explained.
▶ If you list information, that will be considered to be one point and will get only one mark.
▶ Up to two marks may be given for the application of relevant and developed pieces of recalled information. This has to be relevant to the question for full marks to be given.

The following task is intended to help you practise the 8-mark question in the external exam.

2 **To what extent did the Beveridge Report cause the setting up of the Welfare State?** (8 marks)

Your answer should include:

▶ An introduction which mentions the impact of the Beveridge Report and other reasons such as the impact of the Second World War.
▶ A paragraph which discusses the impact of the Beveridge Report.
▶ A paragraph which discusses the impact of the bombing, rationing and evacuation during the Second World War.
▶ A conclusion which is based on the evidence presented and addresses the question.

Planning your answer

▶ In small groups or pairs, brainstorm the impact of the Beveridge Report and other reasons such as the impact of the Second World War.
▶ Group the information into 'Impact of the Beveridge Report' and 'Impact of the Second World War' paragraphs.
▶ Find connections between the different pieces of information and group them together. This will give you a structure for the order in which you talk about the impact of the Beveridge Report and other reasons such as the impact of the Second World War.
▶ Plan an overall response to the question.
▶ Show your plan to your teacher before starting your first draft.
▶ Read through your work carefully and mark any mistakes you spot with a green pen, then correct your work before handing it to your teacher.
▶ Rewrite the final draft of your answer.

Success criteria

Knowledge

▶ Make a judgement about the impact of the Beveridge Report and other reasons such as the impact of the Second World War.
▶ Your answer must provide a balanced account of the impact of the Beveridge Report and other reasons such as the impact of the Second World War.
▶ Up to five marks are given for relevant knowledge used to address the question.
▶ One mark will be given for each accurate point which is properly explained.
▶ You can get a further mark for each point by developing its detail or explanation.
▶ A maximum of three marks are allocated for relevant knowledge used to address the question where only one factor or only one side of the argument is presented.

Structure

▶ Up to three marks can be given for presenting the answer in a structured way, leading to a reasoned conclusion which addresses the question.
▶ One mark may be given for the answer being presented in a structured way. The information should be organised and mention different factors.
▶ One mark may be given for a valid judgement or overall conclusion.
▶ One mark may be given for a reason being provided in support of the conclusion.

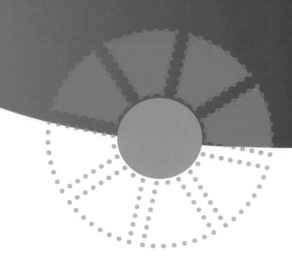

Chapter 16 How successful were the Labour reforms at solving the problems of 'Want' and 'Idleness'?

What is this chapter about?

This chapter is about the setting up of the Welfare State by the Labour Government after the Second World War. This means the government planned to look after the well-being, or welfare, of all its citizens based on need and not contributions. In 1945, the government had to deal with many problems. One of the biggest problems was the poor condition of the country's economy.

By the end this chapter you should be able to:

▶ Describe the Welfare State.
▶ Explain the difficulties faced by the Labour Government in setting up the reforms.
▶ Describe the 1945 Family Allowances Act.
▶ Describe the 1946 National Insurance Act.
▶ Describe the Industrial Injuries Act.
▶ Describe the work of the 1948 National Assistance Board.
▶ Describe nationalisation.
▶ Explain the effectiveness of the Labour reforms for 'Want' and 'Idleness'.

What difficulties did the government face in setting up the Welfare State?

By 1948, the Labour Government had set up most of the services that made up the Welfare State. It was a remarkable achievement given the death and destruction the Second World War had caused to Britain. The economy and essential industries were badly run down. Britain had been forced to sell £1,000 million of foreign investments to pay for the war. The damage done by the Second Word War to the economy of foreign countries meant that there were no markets for Britain's exports. In addition, the number of merchant ships that Britain could trade with were cut due to the war.

Britain also owed a great deal of money to America. She had fought the war with goods and materials from America under a 'Lend-Lease' agreement. Britain was supposed to pay for these at some point and owed America over £3,000 million. She still needed the help given by America but when the war ended, so did the aid. America notified Britain just eight days after the fighting ended that no more materials would be sent without immediate payment. The problems faced by the Labour Government were made worse by a severe winter in 1947–48 and the tension between the Western countries and Russia. It seemed an unwise time to disarm, but the government really needed to reduce its spending on the army.

Some economists and government departments like the Treasury thought that Britain could not afford the Welfare State and wanted to postpone it. But Prime Minister Clement Attlee was determined that Labour would not betray its election promises.

Money was raised in several ways:

▶ Essential industries were nationalised so that the government could firmly control the economy. These included coal, electricity, gas, the railways and waterways, airways and the Bank of England.
▶ Rationing continued on food, fuel and clothing. The choice of consumer goods in shops was still limited.
▶ The economist J.M. Keynes negotiated a further loan from America. Unfortunately, Britain had to pay interest on the loan and that made repayments higher.
▶ Britain received the largest single amount of 'Marshall Aid' of any country – about 26 per cent. This was money from America to help allies against the spread of communism from Russia. They hoped to make countries like Britain well off so as to provide a barrier around communism.

It took a great deal of courage for the Labour Government to push ahead with the reforms in such a situation. Even at the start of the Welfare State it was obvious that paying for it was not going to be easy.

What was the Welfare State?

The Welfare State was a system of state help and benefits. It was started in 1945 by the Labour Government and aimed to do away with the causes of poverty. These had been identified in 1942 by William Beveridge as Want, Disease, Ignorance, Squalor and Idleness.

The Welfare State was different from government help that had existed before for three main reasons:

1 It was a universal scheme that applied to everyone.
2 Benefits were centrally organised and given out by the government.
3 People were now entitled to benefits having paid National Insurance contributions from their pay packets.

The key reforms of the Welfare State were aimed at reducing Want and Disease. Although important acts like the 1944 Education Act and the 1945 Family Allowance Act were passed by the wartime government, the reforms were actually carried out after 1945. It is unlikely these reforms would have been passed without the determination of two women Labour ministers: Eleanor Rathbone and Ellen Wilkinson.

SOURCE 16.1

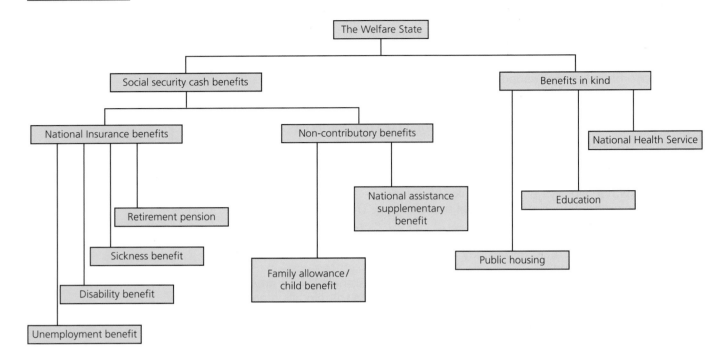

The benefits of a Welfare State

What was the 1945 Family Allowances Act?

Every family was given an allowance of five shillings a week for the second child and every child thereafter under school leaving age. It was paid at the Post Office and was a universal benefit.

What was the 1946 National Insurance Act?

Almost everyone welcomed the new universal insurance scheme. Both Labour and the Conservatives made speeches in favour of it.

Main points of the 1946 National Insurance Act:

▶ Benefits were set up for unemployment, sickness, maternity and widows.
▶ Allowances were paid to guardians/parents in charge of children.
▶ Retirement pensions were paid.
▶ Death grants were given to help with funeral expenses.
▶ Rates of benefit were: 26 shillings a week for the basic rate; 42 shillings for a married man; and 7s 6d extra for the first child.

James Griffiths was the man who was in charge of making Beveridge's dream a reality. He went further than Beveridge had expected and gave pensions to old people at once rather than waiting for a 20 year delay. He also passed the Industrial Injuries Act.

Main points of the 1946 Industrial Injuries Act:

▶ No-fault compensation and payments for injuries and illnesses caused by employment.
▶ Long-term payments for anyone permanently unable to work. This group also got a higher rate of benefit than someone just out of a job.

In 1948, the National Assistance Act set up a Board to help people not covered by the National Insurance Act. Some had found that the benefits were not enough to live on in the long term. Old people, especially, found that their benefits did not keep up with the cost of living.

Main work done by the National Assistance Board:

▶ People had to undergo a 'needs test'.
▶ Provide help to people not covered by the National Insurance Act.
▶ Interview applicants claiming help to assess genuine need.
▶ Provide weekly or one-off payments for needs such as bedding or clothing.

The National Insurance and assistance schemes were a great leap forward in setting a basic standard of living for all. But they needed a great number of government workers to organise and run the system.

SOURCE 16.2

> The family allowance was usually paid to the mother of the family. Why do you think the government did this?

The first family allowance day in Stratford, East London, 6 August 1946

What was nationalisation?

Beveridge had insisted that only full employment could solve the problem of poverty. Without it, social services would only cure the symptoms of poverty, not the causes. The Labour Government was fully committed to the idea of full employment. It fitted in with their idea that the economy should be controlled by the government.

One of the ways in which the government did this was to nationalise certain main industries. Government control of main industries was an important socialist idea. Nationalisation took place as follows:

1946 Bank of England, civil aviation

1947 National Coal Board, cables and wireless

1948 British Transport Commission (road, rail, etc.), electricity

1949 Gas

1950 Iron and Steel.

The government also put in place other important economic policies:

▶ Conversion of war industries to peacetime work
▶ Rapid demobilisation of the workforce serving in the Armed Forces
▶ Regional policy; setting up Development Areas to 'take the work to where the workers are'
▶ Managing demand for goods with government information campaigns, e.g. clothing.

Nationalisation was a mixed success. It kept unemployment very low, but some industries, like coal mining, were very badly run and cost the government money.

How successful were the Labour reforms for 'Want'?

What they did	What they didn't do
National Insurance gave financial help to the unemployed or sick.	Insurance scheme was expensive to run.
Gave pensions to all old-aged people.	Welfare benefits were only 19 per cent of the average industrial wage. This was not enough for people to live on.
Help was given for costs like bedding and funerals.	Many people still lived on incomes below acceptable levels.
National Assistance Boards were set up.	National Insurance benefits only covered people who had made 156 contributions.
National Assistance gave help to all unemployed, sick or elderly not covered by National Insurance.	More people than expected had to apply for National Assistance to get enough money to live on. Most of these were elderly. By 1949, nearly half of the cost of National Assistance went on 'topping up' old age pensions.
Minimal living conditions for unemployed were the same across the whole country.	
Industrial Injuries Act was compulsory for all workers.	National Assistance benefits were 'means tested' which meant many elderly did not apply because they thought there was a stigma to such benefits.
Industrial Injuries Act gave short and long term help.	
Industrial Injuries Act benefits were higher than sickness benefits.	Industrial Injuries benefits were paid by the government, not employers which meant the taxpayer had to pay the cost of poor working conditions.

Activity 1

To what extent were the Labour reforms successful at tackling the problem of Want? You should identify at least two points of view and make three points. Give a judgement on how successful Labour were at tackling the problem of Want. (N5 British AS 1.1/1.2/2.1/2.2/2.3)

How successful were the Labour reforms for 'Idleness'?

What they did	What they didn't do
Despite shortages and massive debts, the Labour Government managed to grow and develop the economy.	Wages and working conditions did not improve a great deal.
Nationalisation of key industries helped to create and maintain job levels.	Some industries like coal were inefficient.
Government control of the economy meant that short-term difficulties for an industry did not lead to job losses.	Some industries did not improve profitability because they were supported by the government.
In Development Areas, unemployment fell from 22 per cent in 1937 to single figures by 1947.	
By 1946, national unemployment was only 2.5 per cent.	

Activity 2

How well did the Labour Government deal with the problem of Idleness? You should draw up a table headed 'Successes' and 'Limits' and put at least two pieces of evidence in your own words. (N4 British AS 1.1/1.2/2.1)

Chapter summary

In this chapter you will have learnt about:
- The Labour Government faced severe problems in setting up the Welfare State.
- The Labour Government helped children with the 1945 Family Allowance Act.
- The Labour Government put Beveridge's insurance scheme into action through the 1946 National Insurance and Industrial Injuries Acts.
- The Labour Government nationalised key industries to help maintain full employment.
- The Labour Government had mixed success in tackling the problems of Want and Idleness.

Activity 3

A spider diagram can help you to summarise the information on the problems experienced by the Labour Government in setting up their reforms in 1945. You can choose to do the planning for this task in pairs or small groups, but it would be a good idea to complete the spider diagram on your own in your workbook or work file. This will give you a learning check on how well you know the information.

Using a large piece of paper, make notes on 'Problems faced by the Labour Government in 1945'.

If you work in threes, one person can read, one person can listen and summarise, and one person can write down the information. Make sure you include at least three pieces of information for each problem identified.

Take a double page in your workbook or work file and record the information you have researched in a colourful and well-presented spider diagram.

Activity 4

Graffiti board

You will need a wall space that can be used as a graffiti board where you can write and record thoughts on the success of the Labour reforms.

Your teacher will give each of you a Post-it note. Write one question or piece of information you know about the Labour reforms tackling Want. Add one question or piece of information you would like to find out about.

Hold a discussion on the comments on the Post-it notes and put the notes onto the graffiti board. When everyone has finished, take another Post-it note and record what you have learnt about the Labour Government's attempts to deal with the problem of Want.

Question practice

NATIONAL 4

Clement Atlee said:

SOURCE A

We now recognise that it is an economic loss to the country to allow, through unemployment or sickness, great numbers of people to be unable to buy things. This is why we need National Insurance.

1 Explain why Atlee thought Britain benefited from National Insurance.
   (N4 British AS 2.2)

Success criteria

You should give one point of information in your own words.

NATIONAL 5

1 **Explain the reasons why the Labour Government found it difficult to set up the Welfare State in 1945. (5 marks)**

This is an 'explain' question. This means you must give five reasons why something did or did not happen. It is not enough to just write down facts no matter how correct they are. You must link each fact back to the question, explaining how that fact did or did not allow something to happen. For this question, this means you need to explain why the conditions in Britain and abroad caused difficulties in the setting up of the Welfare State.

To get you started on your answer, here are some hints:

▸ Explain why the death and destruction of the Second World War caused difficulties in setting up the Welfare State.
▸ Explain why the run-down economy and essential industries caused difficulties in setting up the Welfare State.

▶ Explain why Britain having to sell off foreign assets caused difficulties in setting up the Welfare State.
▶ Explain why the lack of foreign markets for Britain's exports caused difficulties in setting up the Welfare State.
▶ Explain why the severe winter of 1947 caused difficulties in setting up the Welfare State.
▶ Explain why increasing tension between Western Europe and Russia caused difficulties in setting up the Welfare State.

Success criteria

▶ Include five factual pieces of information on why the Labour Government found it difficult.

OR

▶ Include at least three developed pieces of information on why the Labour Government found it difficult.
▶ Give accurate and detailed pieces of information that are properly explained.

2 **Describe the Labour Government's reforms to deal with the problem of Want, 1945–51.** (6 marks)

You would not get a source to help with this question in the exam, but use the following prompt card to help get you started:

Prompt card

▶ 1945, Family Allowance Act
▶ 1946, National Insurance Act
▶ 1946, Industrial Injuries Act
▶ 1948, National Assistance Act
▶ Nationalisation
▶ Full employment policy.

Success criteria

▶ Include six factual pieces of information on the Labour Government's reforms to deal with the problem of Want, 1945–51.

OR

▶ Include at least three developed pieces of information on the Labour Government's reforms to deal with the problem of Want, 1945–51.
▶ Give accurate and detailed pieces of information that are properly explained.

3 **Describe the Labour Government's reforms to deal with the problem of Idleness, 1945–51.** (5 marks)

You would not get a source to help with this question in the exam, but use the following prompt card to help get you started:

Prompt card

▶ Full-employment policy
▶ Nationalisation of main industries
▶ Conversion of war industries to peacetime work
▶ Demobilisation
▶ Regional policy
▶ Managing demand for goods.

Success criteria

▸ Include five factual pieces of information on the Labour Government's reforms to deal with the problem of Idleness.

OR

▸ Include at least three developed pieces of information on the Labour Government's reforms to deal with the problem of Idleness.

▸ Give accurate and detailed pieces of information that are properly explained.

Source A is from a diary by James Griffiths who was the Labour Minister for Social Security from 1945.

SOURCE A

In his report Beveridge warned us that 'freedom from want cannot be forced on a democracy, it must be won by them.' My aim was to provide security with dignity. I considered providing benefits on a sliding scale linked to the cost of living. In the 1940s we fought and won a battle for the cause of social security. We rejoice that the present generation know nothing of the poverty and distress of the nineteen thirties.

4 **Evaluate the usefulness of Source A as evidence of the Labour Government's attempts to deal with the problem of Want, 1945–51.** (6 marks)

Success criteria

▸ For a mark to be given, you must identify an aspect of the source and make a comment that shows how this aspect makes the source more or less useful.

▸ Up to four marks may be given for points about **author**, **type of source**, **purpose** and **timing**.

▸ Up to two marks may be given for your evaluation of the content of the source which you consider are useful in terms of the proposed question. For full marks to be given each point needs to be discretely mentioned and its usefulness explained.

▸ If you list information, that will be considered to be one point and will get only one mark.

▸ Up to two marks may be given for the application of relevant and developed pieces of recalled information. This has to be relevant to the question for full marks to be given.

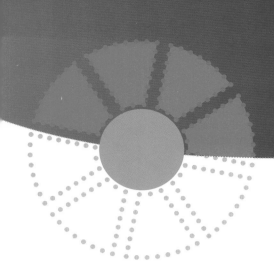

Chapter 17 How far did the Labour welfare reforms solve the problem of 'Disease'?

What is this chapter about?

In 1948 the National Health Service (NHS) came into operation. It was immediately one of the most popular services in the Welfare State. However, it was also one of the most expensive, and from the start, the government struggled to pay for the full cost of the service.

By the end of this chapter, you should be able to:

▶ Describe the role of Aneurin Bevan in building the health service.
▶ Explain why doctors opposed the service at first.
▶ Describe how Bevan overcame opposition.
▶ Assess the success of Labour's NHS reforms.

Who was Aneurin Bevan?

Bevan was the son of a Welsh coal-miner and he also worked as a miner from the age of 13. He soon became an active trade unionist and helped in the General Strike of 1926. From 1929, he was the Labour MP for Ebbw Vale. He was a brilliant speaker and was known for his strong Socialist views. Bevan was Minister of Health between 1945–51. He was responsible for introducing the NHS and trying to solve the post-war housing problems. Bevan resigned as Minister of Health when prescription charges were introduced in 1951.

What role did Bevan play in creating the NHS?

Bevan's biggest problem in setting up the NHS was getting the co-operation of the doctors and dentists. They didn't want to lose their independence and were worried that they would be turned into government workers, sent wherever the government wanted to put them. The Bill for the National Health Service was passed in 1946 with a two-year delay before it was put into practice. Bevan used the time to get the doctors on his side.

Bevan also worked out a plan to deal with the other big problem; getting hold of hospitals for treatment. Before 1948, these were run by a mixture of local authorities and voluntary organisations. Despite opposition, Bevan decided to bring all hospitals into government ownership.

Why were doctors opposed to the NHS?

A lot of hospital workers were keen on the Health Service reforms. By the end of the Second World War, many hospitals needed modernising and to buy new, expensive equipment. They saw the NHS as being their only way of getting what they needed.

The real opposition came from the General Practitioners (GPs). In 1946, an opinion poll showed that 64 per cent of GPs were opposed to Bevan's plans. They believed that his reforms would destroy a doctor's freedom to treat a patient as they wished.

The **British Medical Association** (BMA) organised a fierce campaign of resistance against Bevan.

A former secretary of the BMA, Dr Alfred Cox, attacked Bevan and the NHS reform in 1946:

SOURCE 17.1

I have examined the NHS bill and it looks to me like the first big step towards Nazism as practised in Germany. The medical service there was put under the dictatorship of a 'medical Führer'. This bill will establish the Minister of Health as just such a leader.

From Peter Hennessy, Never Again

How did Bevan win over the doctors?

Bevan had already won over health workers such as dentists, but most GPs remained opposed to the NHS. However, Bevan won over enough doctors by promising:

- Hospital workers would have the buildings and equipment they needed.
- Consultant doctors could continue to treat private as well as NHS patients.
- Doctors would get a salary and the right to earn more money with private patients.
- Each hospital would have some private beds for people who wanted to have private treatment.

This left the GPs isolated against public opinion, which was strongly in favour of the new NHS. By May 1948, Bevan had persuaded a quarter of doctors in England, and over a third of doctors in Scotland and Wales, to sign up for the NHS. At this point organised opposition collapsed and the NHS started working on 5 July 1948.

SOURCE 17.2

SOURCE 17.2

Contemporary cartoon by David Low

Why does the cartoonist think dentists agreed with Bevan's health plans?

How was the NHS organised?

Hospitals were organised into regional groups and run by a Regional Board appointed by Bevan. Each hospital had its own management committee.

GPs were supervised by area Executive Councils. They were allowed to keep some of their independence. Only part of their pay came from direct salary but most of it depended on the number of patients they had.

Local authorities kept their Medical Officers who looked after services like vaccination and child care, and also care for the elderly.

What were the benefits to the people?

People now had access to basic health services free of charge. One historian, Rudolph Klein, said that:

SOURCE 17.3

... the NHS represented 'the jewel in the crown' of Britain's welfare state.

R. Klein in D. Gladstone, The Twentieth-Century Welfare State

SOURCE 17.4

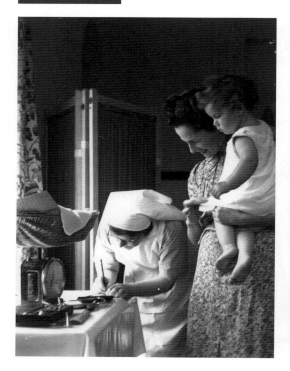

NHS nursing care

SOURCE 17.5

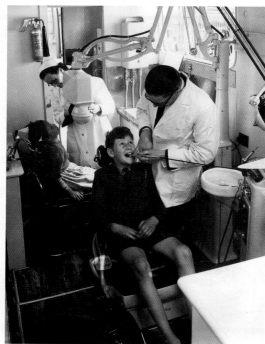

Dental treatment under the NHS

> What difference do you think these services would have made to people's lives?

What were the problems with the NHS?

The government had expected that, at first, there would be a high demand for services. But once people's needs were met, they hoped the costs would quickly drop. However, demand far outstripped government estimates. The cost of prescriptions alone more than doubled in the months after July 1948. The same pattern was repeated in other services such as the dentists and opticians.

For the cash-strapped Labour Government, financing the NHS soon became a real problem. National Insurance health contributions only paid for about 10 per cent of the service's costs, the rest was met out of taxation. Aneurin Bevan was opposed to prescription charges but in 1951 they had to be introduced. Bevan resigned in protest. The bar chart opposite shows the huge increase in welfare spending between 1949 and 1959.

SOURCE 17.6

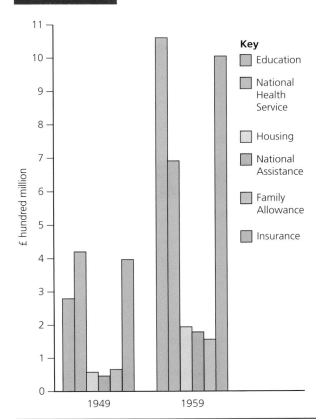

Key
- Education
- National Health Service
- Housing
- National Assistance
- Family Allowance
- Insurance

Welfare spending costs, 1949–59

Bevan's NHS was an enormous organisation. Even today, the NHS is still one of the biggest employers in the UK. However, little attention was paid to the management problems that came with setting up such a new large organisation. There was a lot of confusion about who ran what before the NHS settled down.

How successful were the Labour health reforms?

What they did	What they didn't do
NHS set up in 1948. Free treatment from GPs, dentists, opticians and hospitals. Access to medical services based on need, not ability to pay. Women probably gained most; the group most likely not to pay for medical care either because of cost or putting family needs first. Huge demand for treatment from doctors, dentists and opticians which patients had not been able to afford to pay for previously. Gave out a huge number of prescriptions – seven million per month before the NHS rising to 13.5 million per month in September 1948.	Most of the hospitals were outdated and not fit for purpose. By 1950 the NHS was costing £358 million per year. Most of this cost came out of general taxation. The government was not able to deliver a totally free service – charges were quickly introduced for glasses and dental treatment.

Chapter summary

▶ Aneurin Bevan played a crucial role in setting up the NHS.
▶ Many doctors opposed the NHS because they wanted to keep their independence.
▶ Bevan negotiated a compromise over pay and facilities that allowed the NHS to launch in 1948.
▶ NHS hospitals were run by regional boards and GPs were supervised by executive councils.
▶ Demand for the NHS meant that the government had problems paying for the cost. Some charges for glasses and dental treatment were introduced.

Activity 1

Just a minute

Work in small groups or pairs. Each group should research at least two of the following topics:

▶ Aneurin Bevan
▶ The struggle to win over doctors to the NHS
▶ How Bevan won over the doctors
▶ How the NHS was organised
▶ Problems with paying for the NHS.

After research time, one person in the group will be 'hot-seated' and asked to present their main findings in just one minute.

Other pupils in the class will listen carefully to the presentation. If they hear hesitation, deviation or repetition they can challenge the person in the hot seat. When a challenge happens, the timer is stopped and the teacher or 'judges' will decide whether the challenge is valid, justifying their decision. If the challenge is valid, the person in the 'hot seat' is out and must leave the seat, the group making the challenge gets a point. If the challenge is not valid, the person in the 'hot seat' continues until another challenge is made or the minute is up. If the person manages to stay in the seat for the full minute, they get double points for their group.

Activity 2

Topic triangle

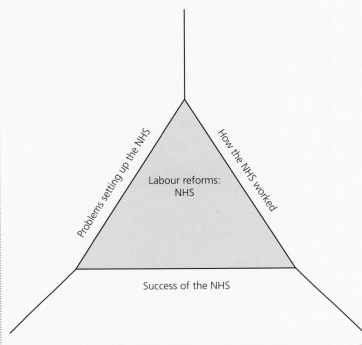

This task is intended to help you summarise the contents of this chapter.

Take a whole page in your workbook or work file.

Draw a small triangle in the middle of your page, then divide the page into three. Look at the template for advice on how to do this.

In the middle of the small triangle, put the heading: 'Labour reforms – NHS'.

On the sides of the triangle, put the headings: 'Problems setting up the NHS', 'How the NHS worked' and 'Success of the NHS'.

Fill up the space around each side of the triangle with key points about how that topic led to social reform. You can use pictures, symbols or writing to make your key points.

Question practice

NATIONAL 4

SOURCE A

It is available to the whole population freely. It is intended that there shall be no limit on the kind of assistance given – the GP service, the specialist, the hospitals, eye treatment, spectacles, dental treatment, hearing facilities.

1 Describe the treatments offered by the NHS from 1948. (N4 British AS 1.1/2.1)

Success criteria

Include at least two points of information, or one point of information that is fully explained, in your own words.

NATIONAL 5

SOURCE A

The NHS reforms in 1948 have been criticised. Doctors were allowed to continue in private practice while working for the NHS. A number of 'pay-beds' were kept in public hospitals. The private sector expanded and fed off the resources of the NHS. The British Medical Association obstructed the setting up of the NHS as much as possible. As late as 1948, doctors were opposed, eight to one, to working in the NHS.

1 How fully does Source A explain the criticisms of the NHS reforms? (6 marks)

Success criteria

▶ Place the source in context by explaining information in the source and applying that information to your own knowledge.
▶ Up to two marks may be given if only the source or recall is given.
▶ Up to three marks may be given for explaining pieces of information from the source.
▶ Up to four marks may be given for explaining pieces of information from your own knowledge which are relevant to the question asked.
▶ Pieces of information from your own knowledge can be used as further explanation of information in the source or as new points.

The following task is intended to help you practise the 8-mark question in the external exam.

2 To what extent was the Labour Government successful in tackling the problem of Disease, 1945–51? (8 marks)

Your answer should include:

▶ An introduction which mentions the success of Labour's NHS reforms and their limitations.
▶ A paragraph which discusses the success of Labour's NHS reforms.
▶ A paragraph which discusses the limitations of the reforms including cost, hospitals, opposition to reforms and prescription charges.
▶ A conclusion which is based on the evidence presented and addresses the question.

Planning your answer

▶ In small groups or pairs, brainstorm the success of Labour's NHS reforms and their limitations including cost, hospitals, opposition to reforms and prescription charges.
▶ Group the information into 'Success of NHS reforms' and 'Limitations of NHS reforms' paragraphs.
▶ Find connections between the different pieces of information and group them together. This will give you a structure for the order in which you talk about the success of Labour's NHS reforms and their limitations.
▶ Plan an overall response to the question.
▶ Show your plan to your teacher before starting your first draft.
▶ Read through your work carefully and mark any mistakes you spot with a green pen, then correct your work before handing it to your teacher.
▶ Rewrite the final draft of your answer.

Knowledge

▶ Make a judgement about the success of Labour's NHS reforms and their limitations.
▶ Your answer must provide a balanced account of the success of Labour's NHS reforms and their limitations.
▶ Up to five marks are given for relevant knowledge used to address the question.
▶ One mark will be given for each accurate point which is properly explained.
▶ You can get a further mark for each point by developing its detail or explanation.
▶ A maximum of three marks are allocated for relevant knowledge used to address the question where only one factor or only one side of the argument is presented.

Structure

▶ Up to three marks can be given for presenting the answer in a structured way, leading to a reasoned conclusion which addresses the question.
▶ One mark may be given for the answer being presented in a structured way. The information should be organised and mention different factors.
▶ One mark may be given for a valid judgement or overall conclusion.
▶ One mark may be given for a reason being provided in support of the conclusion.

Chapter 18 How successful were the Labour reforms at solving the problems of 'Squalor' and 'Ignorance'?

What is this chapter about?

After the Second World War the housing problem was worse than ever. There were not only the pre-war housing slums, but also thousands of homes destroyed by German bombing. The Labour Government made huge efforts to deal with this problem. While they accomplished a lot, they were only partially successful in meeting the demand for houses. Labour also made progress with the problem of Ignorance. From 1947 onwards, they made various education reforms.

By the end of this chapter you should be able to:

▶ Describe the problems the government faced in dealing with the housing shortage.
▶ Describe the 1946 Housing Act.
▶ Describe the 1946 New Towns Act.
▶ Describe the 1947 Town and County Planning Act.
▶ Describe the 1949 Council Act.
▶ Describe the 1944 Education Act.
▶ Assess the success of the Labour reforms for dealing with Squalor.
▶ Assess the success of the Labour reforms for dealing with Ignorance.

What problems did the Labour Government face with housing?

The government faced several problems. The first of these was the fact that there was a lot of slum housing that still existed from before the war. Secondly, many homes had been destroyed during the war.

The scale of the problem faced by the Labour Government was huge.

SOURCE 18.1

Slum housing on Nicholson Street in the Gorbals, Glasgow, circa 1956

SOURCE 18.2

The generally accepted estimate of three to four million houses is a broad indication of the probable housing need during the first 10 to 12 years of the peace.

Aneurin Bevan

There were other problems that would make the meeting of this target a miracle. Housing materials were in very short supply and it was difficult to import materials from abroad because Britain did not have the money to buy all that was needed.

In addition to the shortage of housing materials, there was also a shortage of workers. Many soldiers still had to be demobbed, others were busy trying to pick up their lives when they returned. Bevan was very frustrated at the lack of workers. At one Cabinet meeting, he is said to have angrily demanded: 'Where are all the people I need for my housing work?' Atlee replied: 'Looking for houses, Nye!'

Responsibility for housing was given to the Ministry of Health. Prime Minister Atlee has been criticised for this decision because Bevan had enough to do with building the NHS. Housing was later transferred to a new Ministry of Housing and local government, showing how hard it was for Bevan to give enough time to housing.

The government faced one more problem. They relied on local authorities in England and Wales, and the Scottish Office in Scotland to build the houses for them. Some local authorities, such as the London County Council, were very experienced at house building but some tiny rural councils were not.

What did the Labour Government do to deal with the housing shortage?

The priority was to house the homeless, so the government continued the wartime policy of putting up 'prefabricated' homes. 'Prefabs' as they were known, were ready-made factory built houses that could be quickly slotted together. They were supposed to be temporary houses but some were still being used in the 1990s! They were very popular with their occupants.

From 1946, the government switched priority to building permanent houses. Bevan aimed to build homes not just in quantity, but also in quality. He increased the size of houses and provided toilets upstairs and down. The government also boosted the **subsidy** for council building through the 1946 Housing Act. It would now pay three-quarters of the cost and extended the term of the subsidy from 40 to 60 years.

> **GLOSSARY**
>
> **Subsidy** a loan to pay part or all of the cost

Bevan restricted private house building so that building supplies and labour could be used for council housing. The government also brought back damaged houses into occupation – 600,000 in 1945 alone. The government encouraged the continuation of the wartime policy of taking over houses where needed. Over 70,000 properties were used by councils for tenants in this way. Where possible, Bevan appealed to people to share their homes.

Despite their efforts, the government faced an uphill struggle to meet demand. In 1946 there was a mass **squatter** movement which saw the peaceful occupation of empty properties. In London, the movement was led by the Communist party but elsewhere it was led by people with nowhere else to go. A favourite place to settle was former army camps. By October 1946, an estimated 50,000 people were living in such camps. In most cases, local authorities and the government turned a blind eye to these occupations, hoping that the council building programme would ease the problem.

> **GLOSSARY**
>
> **Squatter** someone who occupies empty property without the owner's permission

Bevan also tried to improve long-term planning for housing. The 1946 New Towns Act tried to solve the problem of overcrowding in the cities by planning new communities. Twelve new towns were planned. The 1947 Town and Country Planning Act gave councils more planning powers and the ability to buy property in areas they wanted to redevelop. Finally, the 1949 Council Act was passed to allow local authorities to buy homes for improvement or conversion; 75 per cent of the costs were available from the government. Private homeowners could get 50 per cent home improvement grants.

SOURCE 18.3

A prefabricated housing estate in London

How successful was Labour in solving the housing problem?

What they did	What they didn't do
For the first time, there was an attempt to nationally co-ordinate a solution to the housing problem.	New towns took time to be built. They did little to ease the immediate housing shortage. In 1951, most of the first phase were still building sites.
The 1946 and 1947 Town and Planning Acts set the basis for town planning for the rest of the century.	In 1947, the currency crisis severely cut the house building programme.
25 new towns were built, today housing over two million people.	Even Bevan called the prefabs 'rabbit hutch' houses!
Nearly 200,000 new homes were built by 1947.	There was still a serious housing shortage in 1951.
Ordinary workers were given good quality homes with space and facilities.	A high demand for housing still existed.
Many prefabs were built. By 1948, nearly 125,000 had been built.	There was almost the same level of homelessness as in 1931.
The Labour Government faced severe shortages and economic problems. They probably did as well as the Liberal Government had done after the First World War.	The 1951 census revealed that the gap between houses and households in Britain was 750,000 more than at pre-war levels.

SOURCE 18.4

The Gorbals rebuilt, Glasgow, circa 1960

What do historians say about the Labour housing reforms?

Most historians agree that Labour had mixed success in dealing with the housing problem.

The historian J.C. Hess has said:

SOURCE 18.5

Bevan's record as regards house-building was poorer than that of his Conservative successor after 1951. But it must not be forgotten that he had to face serious financial and material shortages. In the circumstances Labour's achievement was rather better than is normally painted.

From J.C. Hess in W.J. Mommsen (ed.),
The Emergence of the Welfare State in Britain and Germany (1981)

What progress was made with education (Ignorance)?

The Butler Education Act 1944

The plans to improve education had been made by R.A. Butler, a Conservative politician during the wartime Coalition Government. However, the education reforms are generally included in the Welfare State reforms because it was the Labour Government who put the plans into operation. Ellen Wilkinson, Labour's first Minister of Education deserves a lot of the credit for pushing through the education reforms: critics thought they should be postponed because of Britain's poor economic situation after the war.

Evacuation had shown the need for universal improvement in education. Education was thought to be an important way of fighting poverty, because an educated workforce who could expect better paid jobs.

The Education Act created the post of Minister of Education and a comprehensive education system:

▶ For the first time, three stages of educational development were defined: Primary, Secondary and Further. All education authorities had to provide these stages.

▶ Fees for local authority schools were abolished (although not at direct-grant grammar schools) so there was free education for all up to school leaving age. This was set at 15 from 1945.

▶ In England, schools were divided into grammar schools and secondary moderns; for academic and technical education. In Scotland, schools were divided into senior secondary and junior secondary schools with the same purpose. From the age of 11, children would sit a test to see which school they should go to.

R.A. Butler

The reforms were well received at the time:

SOURCE 18.7

What is the message of the cartoon?

David Low cartoon showing Butler using 'education cement' to help rebuild democracy

Why were the education reforms criticised?

The Education Act was been criticised for setting up social divisions in the education system:

- A two-tier system was created which resulted in the whole adult future of a teenager being decided by the type of school they went to when they were 11 or 12.
- A grammar school (senior secondary) pupil could expect to go on to university and then to a professional job.
- A secondary modern school (junior secondary) pupil would do practical subjects and then do a skilled or semi-skilled trade.
- Critics have argued that young people from poorer backgrounds were discriminated against because they were less likely to go to a grammar or senior secondary school. Therefore, their future choices would be more limited.

The Labour Government was also been criticised for not adding anything new to the wartime Coalition Government's policy.

What problems did education reform face?

Historians like Kenneth Morgan have been puzzled as to why the Labour Party did not do more on education reform when they got into power in 1945. They faced several problems:

The first was one which was common for all the welfare reforms; money. At the end of the Second World War, Britain was so short of money it had to negotiate an emergency loan from America. Most of the money for education went towards funding universal secondary education up to the age of 15 in 1947. Although Scotland already had secondary education for all, in England this was a big change.

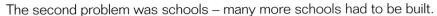

HOW SUCCESSFUL WERE THE LABOUR REFORMS AT SOLVING
THE PROBLEMS OF 'SQUALOR' AND 'IGNORANCE'?

The second problem was schools – many more schools had to be built.

The third problem was the big shortage of teachers. An emergency training scheme had to be put in place to fill the gap. The lack of teachers was a problem the Labour Government spent a lot of time dealing with. George Tomlinson the Minister of Education said in 1947:

SOURCE 18.8

At a pinch you might be able to do without Parliament. You could do without a Minister. You could certainly do without civil servants and local education authorities. Without any or all of them the world might not seem much worse. But if there were no teachers the world would go back to barbarism within two generations.

From Peter Hennessy, *Never Again*

How successful were the Labour education reforms?

What they did	What they didn't do
Secondary education was compulsory until the age of 15.	Support children as individuals. In secondary, there were two types of learner: academic and non-academic. Everyone had to fit into one of these types.
School meals, milk and medical services were provided at every school.	The 11+ exam was socially divisive.
By 1950, 1,176 new schools had been built, 928 of which were primaries.	Provide opportunities for all, especially working-class children.
Pupils no longer had to pay fees to go to grammar schools.	Only 20 per cent could go to grammar schools. Only five per cent of places were available in technical schools. 75 per cent of all school children were classified as non-academic and sent to the low status secondary modern (junior secondary) schools.
Grammar schools provided high quality education that prepared pupils for university. They had good resources, well-trained teachers and small class sizes.	Most grammar school places were taken by middle-class children.
35,000 teachers were trained under the one-year emergency training scheme, 1945–51.	Most working-class children left school at 15 with few qualifications.
	Pupils going to secondary modern (junior secondary) schools had little chance of going on to higher education because their schools concentrated on practical subjects.
	Education reforms did not match up to the investment in health and social security.
	The building of new schools was largely for primary children, the secondary sector was mostly neglected.

Childcare services

The 1948 Children Act tried to give a better service for children who needed government help and protection. Local councils now had to appoint Children's Officers to ensure decent care for children under the authorities' supervision.

Chapter summary

▶ The Labour Government had to deal with a huge housing problem made worse by the destruction of homes from bombing during the Second World War.
▶ Labour's housing reforms only partly deal with the housing problem.
▶ The Labour Government put the 1944 Education Act into operation.
▶ Labour's education reforms set up a comprehensive education system, but were criticised for reinforcing social divisions.

Activity 1

If this is the answer, what is the question?

Below you will find a list of words or names. You have to make up a question that can only be answered by the words on the list. For example, if the name 'Aneurin Bevan' was the answer, a question could be 'Who was the government minister in charge of housing?' Write the question and answer in your work file.

▶ 3–4 million houses
▶ Ministry of Health
▶ Local authorities
▶ Prefabs
▶ 600,000 in 1945
▶ 50,000 people

Activity 2

Summarise this chapter

Write a short summary of this chapter describing the Labour Government's attempts to deal with Squalor. You must describe the success and limitations of the Labour housing reforms in as few sentences as possible. Your question is: 'How successful was the Labour Government, 1945–51, in tackling the problems of Squalor?'

Question practice

SOURCE A

1 *Houses destroyed by bombing.*

2 *Houses needed to reduce overcrowding.*

3 *Houses to meet future increase in the number of families.*

4 *More houses needed in certain areas to cope with population movement.*

5 *Houses needed for slum clearance.*

1 Describe the housing problems faced by the Labour Government after 1945 in your own words. (N4 British AS 1.1/2.1)

Success criteria

You should give at least two points of information in your own words.

1 **Explain the reasons why people were disappointed in the government's efforts to solve the housing problem, 1945–51.** (5 marks)

This is an 'explain' question. This means you must give five reasons why something did or did not happen. It is not enough to just write down facts no matter how correct they are. You must link each fact back to the question, explaining how that fact did or did not allow something to happen. For this question, this means you need to explain why people were disappointed in the government's efforts to solve the housing problem, 1945–51.

To get you started on your answer, here are some hints:

▶ Explain why the number of houses built led to people being disappointed in the government's efforts to solve the housing problem.

▶ Explain why the continuing housing shortage led to people being disappointed in the government's efforts to solve the housing problem.

▶ Explain why the time taken to build the New Towns led to people being disappointed in the government's efforts to solve the housing problem.

▶ Explain why the squatter movement of 1946 led to people being disappointed in the government's efforts to solve the housing problem.

▶ Explain why the cut in the house building programme in 1947 led to people being disappointed in the government's efforts to solve the housing problem.

▶ Explain why the continued problem of homelessness led to people being disappointed in the government's efforts to solve the housing problem.

Sources A and B are about the Labour Government's efforts to solve the housing problem.

SOURCE A

During the 1945 General Election, Labour had promised a massive programme of home building – millions of houses. But after the war, the shortage of materials meant not as many were built. The Government's record of house building was better than that achieved after the First World War. The Government built a mixture of prefabs and permanent homes. However, demand far outstripped supply and the rate of house building did not reach pre-war levels.

SOURCE B

During the 1945 election campaign, Labour had promised to build as many as five million houses. Although the Government made huge efforts, most people agree that Labour had failed to meet expectations. The Government started by building prefabs before moving on to more permanent homes in 1946. They did well in building over 200,000 homes, which was better than after the First World War. The problem was that house building did not keep pace with the rising population.

2 Compare the views in Sources A and B on the Labour Government's efforts to solve the housing problem. (4 marks)

Success criteria

▶ You should interpret evidence from the source.
▶ You should make direct comparisons between the information in the sources.
▶ You can get up to two marks for comparing how far the two sources agree or disagree overall.
▶ You can get up to four marks for making direct comparisons between the information in the two sources.
▶ 'Source A says … and Source B agrees …' will get one mark. A developed comparison: 'Sources A and B agree that Labour promised to build lots of homes. Source A says … and Source B agrees, saying …' will get two marks.

Source C describes problems with the education reforms:

SOURCE C

It is hard to avoid the view that education was an area where the Labour Government failed to provide new ideas or inspiration. However, the new investment at primary level, and the large increase in the school population did pave the way for the educational boom of the fifties and sixties.

3 How fully does Source C describe the problems with the Labour Government's education reforms, 1945–51? (6 marks)

Success criteria

▶ Place the source in context by explaining information in the source and applying that information to your own knowledge.
▶ Up to two marks may be given if only the source or recall is given.
▶ Up to three marks may be given for explaining pieces of information from the source.
▶ Up to four marks may be given for explaining pieces of information from your own knowledge which are relevant to the question asked.
▶ Pieces of information from your own knowledge can be used as further explanation of information in the source or as new points.

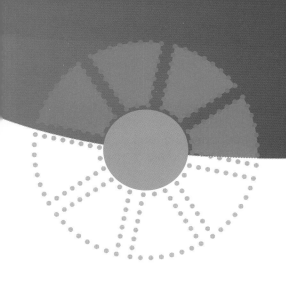

Chapter 19 How successful were the Labour reforms?

What is this chapter about?

The post-war Welfare State made a huge difference to the lives of the people of Britain. From the social security laws of 1945–48 to the setting up of the NHS, there was virtually no part of people's lives where there was no help provided by the government. For the first time, poverty was tackled as a problem to which both social and economic solutions were needed. Despite the limitations of what the Labour government achieved, they deserve credit for their vision and ambition for a better future for Britain's people.

By the end of this chapter you should be able to:

▶ Assess the success of the welfare reforms.
▶ Explain why historians disagree on the success of the reforms.

How successful were Labour's welfare reforms?

We will use the 'five giants' of poverty from the Beveridge Report to help us judge the overall success of Labour's welfare reforms:

	Successes	Problems
Want	The National Insurance, Industrial Injuries and National Assistance Acts meant everyone would be given help 'from the cradle to the grave'.	The schemes needed a lot of people to administer them. Not everyone was covered by the National Insurance Act. Only those people who had paid a certain level of contributions were 'covered'. This meant the 'safety net' did not cover everyone.

	Successes	Problems
Idleness (employment)	The Labour Government actively promoted a policy of full-employment to help support the Welfare State. The Labour Government nationalised key industries to help reach full employment. There was almost full employment after the war despite the post-war economic depression and shortages of goods and materials. Unemployment was around 2.5 per cent.	The British economy and jobs depended heavily on the loans and aid from America. Women found themselves out of jobs when demobbed servicemen came home. Many women were happy to become housewives again but some found themselves excluded from jobs that they would have liked to continue doing.
Disease	The National Health Service Act 1946 gave free medical, dental and eye services to all. The NHS was a huge improvement in the lives of ordinary people, especially women.	Many of the hospitals were old and not suitable for modern health care. Financial pressures on the government meant that most old hospitals were not replaced. The building of new hospitals did not really begin until the 1960s. The NHS was a victim of its own success. So many people used the NHS that it became too expensive for the government to fund out of taxes alone. Prescription charges were introduced in 1951.
Squalor (housing)	It was a main aim of the Labour Government. Bevan, the minister in charge, made sure that prices for building goods and labour were not allowed to become too expensive. This encouraged more building. The New Towns Act, 1946, planned for twelve new towns. The 1949 Council Act gave help to councils to build more council houses. Private homeowners were given help to pay for home improvements. Between 1948 and 1951, around 200,000 homes a year were built. The number of houses built does not compare with the amount built in the 1930s or 1950s, but the Labour Government made real progress at a time when it was short of materials, workers and money.	Many of the houses built were temporary buildings – prefabs. Many families, especially in London, were forced to squat illegally. The government even had to make use of aerodromes which had housed servicemen. There was not enough housing to cope with the demobilisation of nearly five million servicemen and women.

	Successes	Problems
Ignorance (education)	The Butler Education Act, 1944, was a radical advance in education. It raised the school leaving age. An appropriate education was provided for every school pupil. An ambitious school building programme was initiated.	In practice, the Education Act was not fair. Few working-class children had the chance to go to an academic school. The type of school you went to tended to affect your later opportunities for jobs. There was no attempt to solve differences in educational provision across the country. The school building programme concentrated on primary schools to cope with the 'baby boom'. Only 250 secondary schools had been built by the 1950s.

What have historians said about the welfare reforms?

Historians have disagreed about how successful the Labour welfare reforms were.

In favour of the Labour reforms

SOURCE 19.1

Poverty was not abolished, but there is no doubt that the number of people seriously lacking in food, clothing, shelter and warmth was substantially reduced compared with the 1930s (or indeed any other period).

From P.J. Madgewick, et al, British Political History

SOURCE 19.2

It created a system of universally available social insurance, which provided minimum incomes and pensions to those subject to ill-health, industrial accidents, disablement and old age.

From D. Coates, The Labour Party and the Struggle for Socialism

SOURCE 19.3

The fifth of July 1948 was welfare state day. The Health Service came into being and the new social security laws came into force. For many, life was never the same again. It was simply better. None of the frustrations, disappointments or cash crises in subsequent years can detract from that.

From Peter Hennessy, Never Again

Against the Labour reforms

One historian, Corelli Barnett, believes that the Welfare State only succeeded in crushing individual responsibility and creating dependency on the state. Barnett also believes that Bevan and the Labour Government failed to work out properly how much the NHS and other services would cost:

SOURCE 19.4

Why did Bevan and his advisers completely fail to carry out an analysis of the likely demands, along with a calculation of the resources needed? Could it be that, given Britain's precarious finances, even a Cabinet dedicated to the 'New Jerusalem' might have hesitated if presented with a realistic estimate of the cost of the NHS?

Corelli Barnett

Historians seem to disagree partly because they judge the reforms of the Labour Government, 1945–51 on different criteria. Some look at the social benefits, others at the cost. All historians have the benefit of hindsight.

One historian believes that the Labour reforms were a success because they were trying something new:

SOURCE 19.5

The social reforms of the Labour Government were a great improvement on what had gone before, but they were only a first step. The post-war Labour Governments can claim to have established a 'welfare state' because they set up the universal provision of healthcare, social security and education. It was a new approach to the use of the power of the state in the interests of social justice for the mass of the population.

From P. Thane, The Foundations of the Welfare State

Chapter summary

▶ The Labour Government had mixed success in dealing with the 'five giants' of poverty.

▶ Historians have criticised and praised the achievements of the Labour Government.

▶ Despite problems with the reforms, the Labour Government, 1945–51 is to be praised for its attempt to provide universal care 'from the cradle to the grave'.

Activity 1

Summarise this chapter

Put the heading: 'Labour's welfare reforms, 1945–51' in your workbook or work file. Draw a table like the one below and fill in the blanks. Remember that your table will need to be larger to include all your information. The first box has been filled in for you.

Labour's welfare reforms, 1945–51	
Policy	**Government action and progress made**
Full employment	*Unemployment rarely rose above 2 per cent of the workforce.*
Nationalisation	
National Health Service	
Housing	
Education	

Social security benefits:
    Unemployment
    Sickness
    Industrial Injury
    National Assistance	

Activity 2

Mind mapping

Put the heading 'What do historians think about the Labour reforms?' in your workbook or work file. Create a mind map of 'praise for the reforms', 'criticisms of the reforms' and 'my opinion on the Labour reforms'.

Question practice

NATIONAL 4

SOURCE A

Despite criticisms, the Labour Welfare reforms had real success. The setting up of the NHS, was probably the most important because it provided free medical care for the first time. Labour also created new opportunities for young people with its education reforms. Also, Labour worked hard to build high quality homes for all.

1 **Describe the successes of the Labour Welfare reforms, 1945–51.** (N4 British 2.1)

Success Criteria

You should make two relevant, factual points or one developed point that describes Labour's successes.

NATIONAL 5

Source A is by historian Peter Murray, writing in 2006:

SOURCE A

The welfare state set up by the 1945–1951 Labour Government is generally recognised as being very important in the development of social reform. The term 'welfare state' represented a new idea on how the government should relate to the people. It was a turning point in that the government took responsibility at a national level, to provide social security for the whole population. This meant that not only the poorest sections of society, but everyone could benefit from welfare support, particularly family allowances and the National Health Service.

1 How useful is Source A as evidence of the success of the 1945–51 Labour reforms? (6 marks)

Success criteria

▶ For a mark to be given, you must identify an aspect of the source and make a comment which shows how this aspect makes the source more or less useful.
▶ Up to four marks may be given for points about **author**, **type of source**, **purpose** and **timing**.
▶ Up to two marks may be given for your evaluation of the content of the source which you consider useful in terms of the proposed question. For full marks to be given each point needs to be discretely mentioned and its usefulness explained.
▶ If you list information, that will be considered to be one point and will get only one mark.
▶ Up to two marks may be given for the application of relevant and developed pieces of recalled information. This has to be relevant to the question for full marks to be given.

The following task is intended to help you practise the 8-mark question in the external exam.

2 To what extent were Labour's welfare reforms successful in dealing with the 'five giants' of poverty? (8 marks)

Your answer should include:

▶ An introduction which mentions the success of Labour's welfare reforms and their limitations.
▶ A paragraph which discusses the success of Labour's welfare reforms.
▶ A paragraph which discusses the limitations of the reforms.
▶ A conclusion which is based on the evidence presented and addresses the question.

Planning your answer

▶ In small groups or pairs, brainstorm the success of Labour's welfare reforms and limits of the reforms' successes.
▶ Group the information into 'Success of reforms' and 'Limits of reforms' paragraphs.
▶ Find connections between the different pieces of information and group them together. This will give you a structure for the order in which you talk about the success of Labour's welfare reforms and limits of the reforms' successes.
▶ Plan an overall response to the question.
▶ Show your plan to your teacher before starting your first draft.
▶ Read through your work carefully and mark any mistakes you spot with a green pen, then correct your work before handing it to your teacher.
▶ Rewrite the final draft of your answer.

Success criteria

Knowledge

▶ Make a judgement about the success of Labour's welfare reforms and their limitations.
▶ Your answer must provide a balanced account of the success of Labour's welfare reforms and the limitations of the reforms.

> ▶ Up to five marks are given for the relevant use of knowledge to address the question.
> ▶ One mark will be given for each accurate point that is properly explained.
> ▶ You can get a further mark for each point by developing its detail or explanation.
> ▶ A maximum of three marks are allocated for relevant knowledge used to address the question where only one factor or only one side of the argument is presented.
>
> **Structure**
> ▶ Up to three marks can be given for presenting the answer in a structured way, leading to a reasoned conclusion which addresses the question.
> ▶ One mark may be given for the answer being presented in a structured way. The information should be organised and mention different factors.
> ▶ One mark may be given for a valid judgement or overall conclusion.
> ▶ One mark may be given for a reason being provided in support of the conclusion.

Conclusion

By 1951, the reforms that made up the Welfare State had been put into practice. The Labour Party deserves much of the credit for the Welfare State: it was its determination that drove through the reforms despite political opposition, a poor economy and international problems. But the Labour Government also built on the policies of the Liberals and Conservatives. They too had been greatly concerned with improving the lives of people in need through health, housing and education.

The achievement of the Labour Government and the Welfare State by 1951 was clear: for the majority of people, life had greatly improved. In 1950, Seebohm Rowntree did a third study of York. He found that old people still struggled, but that poor pay, overcrowding, unemployment and poverty were not as serious as they once were. Even for the elderly, their lives were more dignified and comfortable than ever before.

Government power and control over people's lives greatly increased in the period, 1890–1951. But so did expectations of a government's responsibility to help its citizens. In particular, the Second World War was a real turning point in changing people's attitudes towards a government's social responsibility. The Beveridge Report rightly deserves the credit for focusing public attention on how best to tackle the problems of poverty.

Ever since the creation of the Welfare State people have continued to argue about how help should be given to those in need and how best to cope with issues like the following:

▶ Should flat rate benefits, like the Family Allowance, be given to everyone, even if they don't need it?
▶ Have state benefits made people too dependent on government help?
▶ How do you decide when a person is 'in need'?
▶ Should the definition of poverty change as standards of living rise?
▶ How do you decide the right levels of benefit so that the benefit prevents poverty but still provides an incentive to work?
▶ Should the Welfare State be more selective in whom it helps?

We may never find ideal answers to these questions. But the reforms of 1890–1951 have left a permanent mark on our society. We take it for granted that help should be given to those in need and that the government should give state benefits. Despite changes to the Welfare System in recent years, we remain a society giving help 'from the cradle to the grave'.

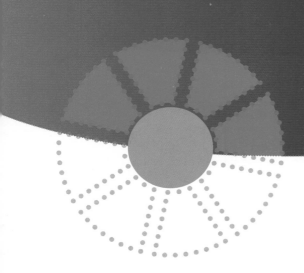

Glossary

A

Able-bodied fit and healthy

B

Barbarism animal-like behaviour

Boers farmers in South Africa descended from Dutch settlers

Borstals youth detention centres

British Medical Association the doctor's professional organisation

By-election an election for an MP in between general elections

C

Citizen a person with rights and responsibilities

Civilian private citizen

Coalition government a government made up of more than one political party

Constitutional monarchy a country that is ruled by a king or queen, but run by an elected government

D

Demobilisation return of women and men who served in the armed forces to civilian life

Deterioration to get worse

E

Economy Britain's trade and industry

F

Friendly Society a partnership association for the purposes of insurance, pensions, savings or banking

G

Grammar schools selective schools based on academic tests

I

Indoor relief help given to the poor in a workhouse or poorhouse
Infirmity physical or mental weakness
Initiate set up
Invalid someone sick or medically unfit
Investigator researcher

J

Juvenile courts special courts for young people

L

Labour exchange a job centre

M

Maxim a statement or saying that aims to sum up a general experience or idea
Merchant ship ship carrying food and trade supplies
Mutual a partnership with others for joint benefit

O

Outdoor relief help given to the poor in their own homes

P

Parish an area of Britain based around the local church
Parliament Britain's decision and law-making body made up of the House of Commons and the House of Lords
Pauper a very poor person in a workhouse
Politician someone who is elected to represent a group of people (usually a political party)
Prescription medicine given by a doctor/dentist
Principle main idea or belief

R

Rationing sharing out food/materials equally
Reeking stinking

S

Salvation Army Christian organisation known for their work in helping those in poverty
Sanitary inspector someone employed by the local council to inspect health and housing
Slum very poor, overcrowded housing
Socialism the idea that the resources and wealth of a country should be shared among its people
Social security government payments preventing poverty
Squalor extremely poor living conditions
Squatter someone who occupies empty property without the owner's permission
Stigma a mark of disgrace or shame
Subsidy a loan to pay part or all of the cost

T

Tax money deducted from wages to pay for government services

Trade union an organisation representing workers' rights

Trespass to go on land or property without permission

Tuberculosis an infectious bacterial lung disease

U

Unemployment joblessness

W

Welfare reform the help given to resolve social problems, e.g. poverty

Welfare State the series of social reforms between 1945 and 1951 that aimed to provide care for people in need 'from the cradle to the grave'

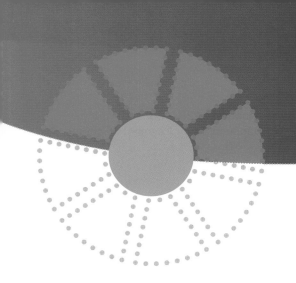

Index

A

Asquith, Herbert 75
assignments
   National 4 vi–viii
   National 5 v–vi

B

Bevan, Aneurin 117–19, 138
Beveridge Report 96, 101–4, 143
Beveridge, William 101–4
Boer War 32–5
bombing attacks 92–4
Booth, Charles 25–6, 29, 55
Booth, William 22
British Empire 4–5, 32
budgets, 1909 74
Butler, R. A. 130–3, 132

C

charities 19–22, 88
Children Act (1948) 134
Children's Charter 50–2
Churchill, Winston 41–2, 43,
   79, 90
clothes rationing 94–5, 109
Co-operative Societies 19
Committee on Physical
   Deterioration 35, 49
communism 109
community spirit 92–4
conscription 95
Conservative Party 39, 74
constitutional monarchy 6

D

doctors, and the National Health
   Service 118
DORA (Defence of the Realm Act
   1914) 85

E

economic depressions 6–7
economy
   1900 6–7
   post-First World War 86–7
   Second World War 96
   post-Second World War 108–9
education 130–3
Education Act (1944) 131–2, 138
elections, 1910 75
employment 139
   see also unemployment
evacuation 91–2

F

Family Allowance Act 110
family allowances 96, 102, 111
First World War
   welfare reforms 85–6
'five giants' of poverty 102, 105,
   137–9
food rationing 85, 94–5, 109
Friendly Societies 18, 63

G

government
   role of 6, 65

   Second World War 90–1
Griffiths, James 110

H

Hardie, Keir 64
health care 96, 102
health insurance 62–5
Hill, Octavia 20
hospitals 118, 138
House of Lords 74–6
housing 5–6, 126–30, 138

I

idleness
   and Labour reforms 113
   see also 'five giants' of poverty
Industrial Injuries Act 110–11
Industrial Revolution 5

K

Keynes, J. M. 96, 109

L

Labour Exchange Act 66
labour exchanges 66, 69
Labour Party 6, 38, 39, 40, 56,
   104, 108, 143
Labour reforms
   disease 117–22
   squalor and ignorance 126–34
   successes 137–40
   want and idleness 108–14
Liberal Party 38, 39, 40–4, 56

Liberal reforms 40–4
  limitations 78–9
  opposition to 73–6
  successes 79, 81
  views of 79–81
  see also Children's Charter;
    Labour Exchange Act; Medical
    Inspection Act; National
    Insurance Act; old age
    pensions; Schools Meals Act;
    welfare reforms
Lloyd George, David 41, 42–3,
  56–7, 62, 65, 74, 79, 86

M

MacDonald, Ramsay 87
Marshal Aid 109
maternity grants 102
means test 87, 96
Medical Inspection Act 49–50, 51
Ministry of food 85, 94–5

N

National Assistance Board 111
National Efficiency 35
National Health Service 102,
  117–22, 138
National Health Service Act (1946)
  138
National Insurance Act (1911)
  62–5, 66–9, 79, 110, 137
nationalisation 109, 111–12, 139
naval arms race 73
New Towns Act (1946) 128, 138

O

old age pensions 55–9, 73, 96, 102

P

Parliament Act 75–6
pensions
  see old age pensions
Poor Law 10–15, 19
poorhouses 10–15
poverty
  1900 7–8
  definition 2
  and Liberal reforms 78–82
  Poor Law 10–14
  studies on 25–9
power 4–5
prefabs 128–9, 138

R

Rathbone, Eleanor 109
rationing 94–5, 109
Rowntree, Seebohm 25, 27–9, 143

S

Salvation Army 19, 21–2
savings banks 19
Schools Meals Act (1906) 48–9, 51
Second World War
  welfare reforms 90–8
self-help 17–19, 41, 49, 50, 51
Smiles, Samuel 17–18
social reforms 35, 38–44
  see also Labour reforms; Liberal
    reforms; welfare reforms
socialism 39

squatters 128, 138
Supplementary Payments Scheme
  96

T

taxes 73, 85
teacher shortage 133
trade slump (1929) 86–7
trade unions 39, 63

U

unemployment 86–8, 102
  see also employment
unemployment benefit 87–8
unemployment reforms 66–9
United States of America (USA)
  96, 108–9, 132

W

want
  and Labour reforms 112
wealth 4–5
wealth distribution 74
welfare reforms
  post-First World War 85–9
  Second World War 90–8
  see also Labour reforms; Liberal
    reforms
Welfare State 1–2, 79–80, 101–4,
  108–9, 143
widows 102
Wilkinson, Ellen 109, 131
women
  in the workforce 95, 139
workhouses 10–15